Life in Colonial America

Religion in Colonial America

George Capaccio

Cavendish Square
New York

Published in 2015 by Cavendish Square Publishing, LLC
243 5th Avenue, Suite 136, New York, NY 10016

First Edition

Website: cavendishsq.com

CPSIA Compliance Information: Batch #WS14CSQ

Library of Congress Cataloging-in-Publication Data
Capaccio, George.
Religion in colonial america / by George Capaccio.
pages cm. — (Life in colonial America)
Includes index.
ISBN 978-1-62712-888-9 (hardcover) ISBN 978-1-62712-890-2 (ebook)
1. United States — Religion — To 1800 — Juvenile literature. 2. United States — History — Colonial period, ca. 1600 - 1775 — Juvenile literature. 3. Religion — Juvenile literature. I. Capaccio, George. II. Title.

BL2525.C36 2015
200.973—d23

Editorial Director: Dean Miller
Editor: Fletcher Doyle
Senior Copy Editor: Wendy A. Reynolds
Art Director: Jeffrey Talbot
Designer: Joseph Macri and Douglas Brooks
Production Editor: David McNamara
Production Manager: Jennifer Ryder-Talbot

The photographs in this book are used by permission through the courtesy of: Cover photo by Ron and Patty Thomas/The Image Bank/ Getty Images; Medioimages/Photodisc/Getty Images, 4; © Mary Evans Picture Library/Alamy, 5; © Alexei Fateev/Alamy, 6; Album/ Prisma/Album/SuperStock; 8–9, Stock Montage/Archive Photos/Getty Images, 10; Leemage/Universal Images Group/Getty Images, 11; Archive Photos/Getty Images, 13; DEA/G. Dagli Orti/De Agostini/Getty Images, 14; © Charles Walker/TopFoto/The Image Works, 16; Image Asset Management Ltd./SuperStock, 19; SuperStock/SuperStock, 20–21; © North Wind/North Wind Picture Archives, 22; © North Wind/North Wind Picture Archives, 24–25; © North Wind Picture Archives/The Image Works, 26; © North Wind/North Wind Picture Archives, 28; © North Wind Picture Archives/The Image Works, 32; © North Wind Picture Archives/The Image Works, 33; Bridgeman Art Library, London/SuperStock, 34; © North Wind Picture Archives/Alamy, 37; © North Wind Picture Archives/ The Image Works, 38; Increase Mather/File:CasesofConscience1st.jpg/Wikimedia Commons, 42; Album/Prisma/Album/SuperStock, 44; File:Assassinat de Coligny et massacre de la Saint-Barthélemy.jpg./Wikimedia Commons, 47; © North Wind/North Wind Picture Archives, 48; Stock Montage/Archive Photos/Getty Images, 50; © North Wind Picture Archives/The Image Works, 51; © The Print Collector/Alamy, 54; Colin Weston/Photographer's Choice RF/Getty Images, 56; LTL/Universal Images Group/Getty Images, 60; © The Art Gallery Collection/Alamy, 62; © North Wind/North Wind Picture Archives, 65; Hulton Archive/Getty Images, 66.

Printed in the United States of America

Contents

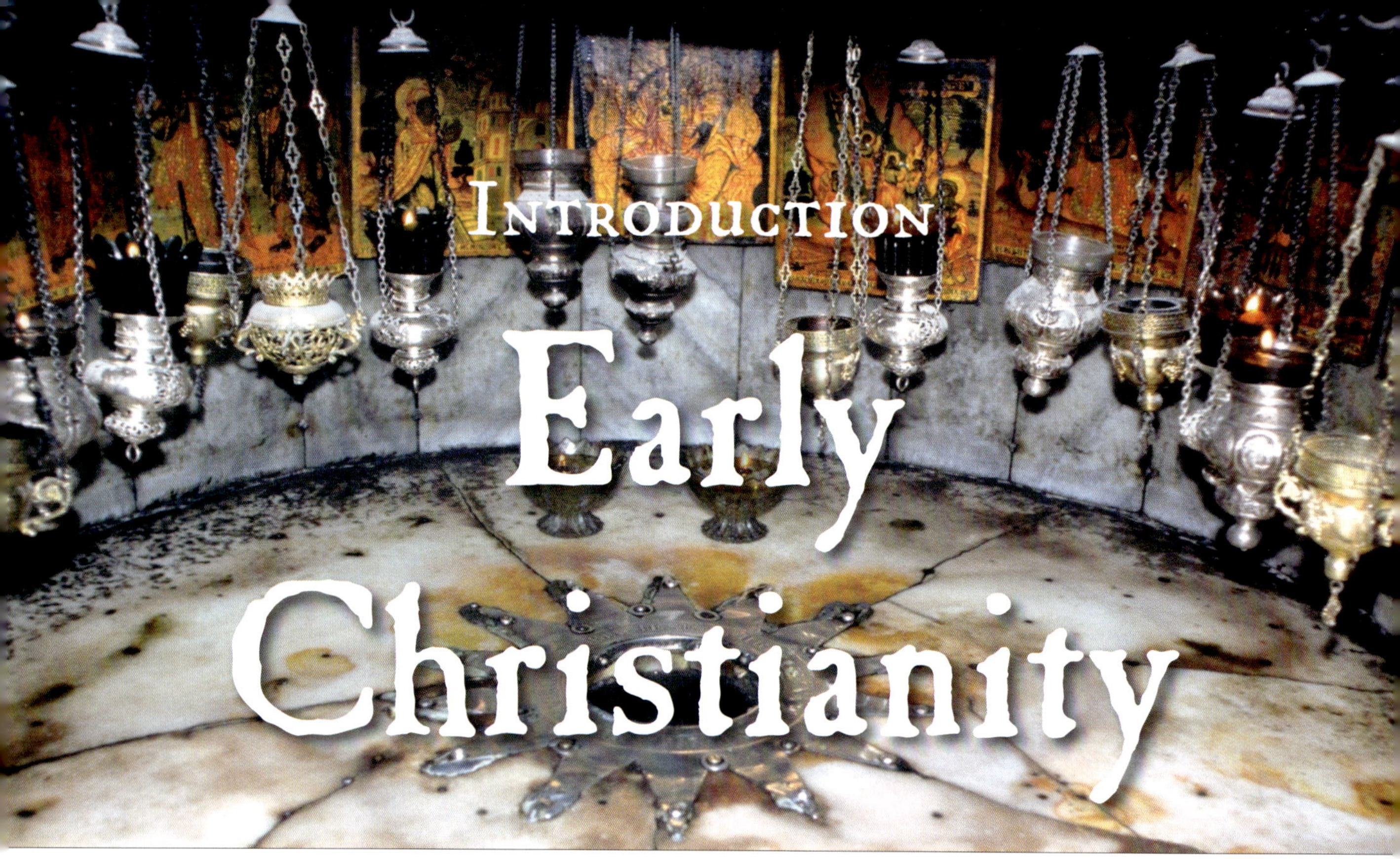

Introduction

Early Christianity

Christianity is one of the world's oldest religions. Two of its main branches are Catholicism and Protestantism, each of which represents alternative ways of organizing the spiritual life of a community while providing spiritual guidance to individual members. Despite their differences, both forms of Christianity base their teachings on the Bible and the life of Jesus Christ, a first-century Jewish preacher whose **disciples**, or followers, eventually became known as Christians. According to **Gospel** accounts in the Bible's New Testament, Jesus was born in the town of Bethlehem, which is about 6 miles (9.6 km) south of Jerusalem, one of the oldest and holiest cities in the world.

Jerusalem is located in the Middle East, the birthplace of three major religions: Christianity, Islam, and Judaism. At the time of Jesus' birth, the Middle East was part of the Roman Empire. The Romans had their own religion and were generally hostile toward those who embraced Christianity. During the church's first three hundred years, Roman authorities periodically oppressed Christians, sometimes by condemning them to death.

Despite the Roman Empire's longstanding intolerance toward Christianity, a dramatic turning point came in the year 313 when the Roman emperors Constantine and Licinius signed the Edict of Milan. This historic document officially ended the persecution of Christians and granted religious freedom to all those who lived within the boundaries of the Empire.

The edict states, "we thought … those regulations pertaining to the reverence of the Divinity ought certainly to be made first, so that we might grant to the Christians and others full authority to observe that religion which each preferred. … And since these Christians are known to have possessed not only those places in which they were accustomed to assemble, namely the churches … you will order to be restored, without any hesitation or controversy at all, to these Christians."

Half a century later, Christianity, once an outlawed and forbidden religion, became the established religion of the Roman Empire.

By the fifth century, the western half of the Empire had disintegrated into separate warring states, but the religion it had recognized and formally adopted continued to grow in power and influence. For nearly 1,500 years, the Roman Church dominated the spiritual life of Western Europe, and greatly influenced the art, customs, architecture, and belief systems of Western civilization. The term "Roman Catholic" was not generally used until the sixteenth century when competing branches of Christianity began to develop, each with its own claim on the basic teachings and practices of the religion.

Perpetua and her servant Felicitas were third-century Christians who refused to give up their faith. A Roman governor sentenced them to death in a North African arena.

Chapter One

The Protestant Reformation

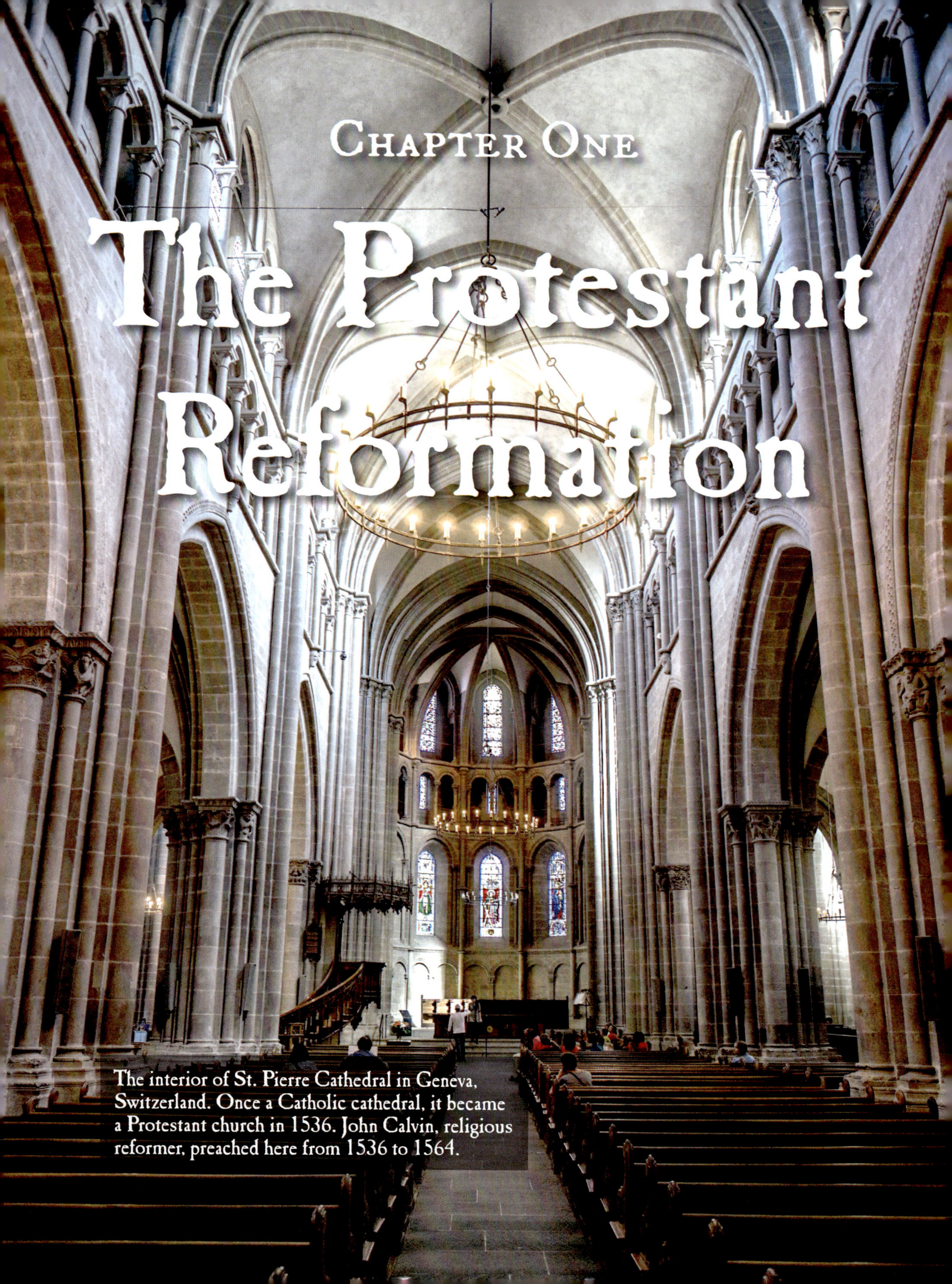

The interior of St. Pierre Cathedral in Geneva, Switzerland. Once a Catholic cathedral, it became a Protestant church in 1536. John Calvin, religious reformer, preached here from 1536 to 1564.

"The pope does very well when he grants remission to souls in **purgatory**, not by the power of the keys, which he does not have, but by way of intercession for them."
—No. 26 of Martin Luther's 95 Theses.

Over the centuries, the Church accumulated great wealth, vast amounts of land, and political power. It also developed a complex **bureaucracy** and a hierarchical structure, with the pope as the spiritual head of the Church and the ultimate authority in spiritual matters. At times, the Church lost sight of its spiritual mission and became entangled in the political intrigues of European monarchs, supporting the military campaigns of various rulers and launching holy wars against people considered to be enemies of Christian countries.

The Roman Catholic Church also became involved in corrupt practices for obtaining the money it needed to maintain its power and influence, and the expensive lifestyles of many church leaders. One such practice involved charging people to view "**holy relics**." These were supposed to be authentic materials associated with the life of a particular saint or even Jesus himself, such as straw from the manger where he was born, or pieces of wood from the cross on which he was crucified.

One of the most corrupt practices was the selling of **indulgences**. In the

Roman Catholic Church, committing a **sin** created a debt that would have to be repaid, either in this life or the next. While a person could be forgiven for his sins, this forgiveness did not by itself cancel the debt. After death, the forgiven person would still have to suffer punishment. How long the punishment lasted, in the next life, depended on the good works a person performed while alive.

But during the Middle Ages (which lasted from about the fifth century to the fifteenth century) the Catholic Church offered an alternative way to shorten the duration of a person's punishment in the next life: by giving indulgences. An indulgence is the granting of a sort of reprieve, or "reduced sentence." The original purpose of indulgences was to help people obtain the **salvation** of their souls. However, in time, the practice became tied up with the exchange of money for goods or services. Once money entered the picture, greed soon followed, and members of the clergy began selling indulgences to Christians. For the right price, a person could buy his way out of a certain amount of time in Purgatory—the place after death where those whose sins have been forgiven must temporarily suffer before going to Heaven.

Martin Luther's 95 *Theses*

By the 16th century, there was growing dissatisfaction with the Roman Catholic Church. People living in Europe resented the corruption of church officials, the Church's increasing wealth and power, and its interference in political matters. Some Christians went further and began to openly condemn the Church and to call for its reform. One of the most outspoken reformers was Martin Luther, a German pastor, monk, and **theologian** whose passionate objection to the selling of indulgences led him to openly rebel against this practice. Legend has it that on October 31, 1517, he nailed a collection of his controversial religious views—called the *95 Theses*—on the door of the Castle Church in the university town of Wittenberg, Germany. (Scholars disagree about whether Luther actually nailed his *95 Theses* to the church door. A more likely scenario is that he sent them to certain church officials. When they failed to respond, Luther shared his document with close friends and colleagues.)

Luther's *95 Theses* was a list of statements, written in Latin, which detailed

In 1450 German inventor Johann Gutenberg revolutionized the printing process. Thanks to his innovations, large numbers of manuscripts could be printed in a short period of time.

the author's concern regarding the corruption of the Catholic Church and his strong desire for radical change. Luther hoped his statements would serve as the starting point for a discussion with other scholars. He probably didn't anticipate the uproar his *95 Theses* would cause. Once they were translated from Latin into German, they were read widely by people first in Germany, then throughout Europe, and eventually in England.

Martin Luther

When Martin Luther was born in Germany in 1483, the Roman Catholic Church was the most powerful institution in Western Europe. As a young man, Martin studied to become a lawyer. But one summer afternoon, during a thunderstorm, he was nearly struck by a bolt of lightning. This close call frightened him so much that he prayed to St. Anne—one of the saints recognized by the Church. He promised her that he would become a monk instead of a lawyer if she spared his life.

Martin Luther nails his *95 Theses* to the door of the Castle Church in Wittenberg, Germany.

After getting home safely, Martin kept his word. He dropped out of the university and entered the local monastery. During his monastery training, Martin became increasingly disillusioned with the Church, especially after he visited Rome and saw how wealthy and corrupt the Church leadership had become.

By openly attacking the Catholic Church, Martin Luther triggered a series of events that would end the dominance of the Church and push western Europe into the modern age.

Historians consider the widespread publication of Luther's *95 Theses* the beginning of the **Protestant Reformation**, and the birth of Protestantism as an alternative form of Christianity. Thanks to the invention of a revolutionary new printing process in 1450 by Johann Gutenberg, a German goldsmith, Martin Luther and his associates were able to publish numerous documents critical of the Church. Contrary to the Church's teaching, Luther believed that faith alone is enough to guarantee a person's salvation after death. In his writings, he argued that people did not need the ceremonies and **sacraments** of the official Church in order to be "saved." Furthermore, he said, the Bible—not the Catholic pope—is the ultimate authority in religious matters.

Portrait of John Calvin (1509–1564), French theologian, writer, and pastor during the Protestant Reformation.

These were extremely radical and dangerous ideas for the times in which Luther lived. In 1520, Pope Leo called upon Martin Luther to withdraw forty-one of his criticisms. When Luther refused, the pope excommunicated him, and the disagreement turned personal.

Luther wrote in 1545 that "... doctrinal agreement ... is utterly impossible unless the pope has his papacy abolished. Therefore avoid and flee those who seek the middle of the road. ... There can be no compromise."

Martin Luther's loss of membership in the Church was not enough to stop the movement he had begun.

John Calvin and the Doctrine of Predestination

The Protestant Reformation may have begun with Martin Luther's singular act of defiance, but other critics were also influential in ending the dominance of the Roman Catholic Church. One of them was John Calvin, a French lawyer who had to escape from France because of his relationship with opponents of the Roman Catholic Church. At that time, the king of France and the French government were loyal Catholics who did not tolerate the spread of Protestant ideas. Proponents of these ideas were labeled **heretics** and could be brought to trial and, in some cases, executed.

The Anglican Church

The word "Anglican" means "of England." The origins of Anglicanism go back as far as the sixth century in England. Over the centuries, the Anglican Church developed under the jurisdiction of the Roman Catholic Church. But in the 1530s, King Henry VIII wanted to separate the English Church from the authority of the pope in Rome. Under the Act of Supremacy passed in **Parliament**, Henry replaced the pope as head of the Anglican Church.

John Calvin agreed with much of Luther's teachings, but he had no desire to start a new church. He believed it was possible to return the Catholic Church to the purity and simplicity of its earliest beginnings. Like Martin Luther, Calvin preached the importance of faith for personal salvation. He also taught the doctrine of **predestination**. According to this principle, God has already decided who will go to Heaven and who will go to hell. Therefore, said Calvin, there is no such thing as free will. No matter how good a person is, he can do nothing to change his fate, which only God knows. However, if an individual performs good works and lives a moral life, this is a reliable sign that he or she is one of the "saved" whom God has chosen.

John Calvin envisioned an ideal community made up of people who had been saved by the grace of God. It was this vision that inspired the first migration of English settlers to North America. Their greatest goal was to establish the sort of community Calvin had in mind. We know them today as the **Pilgrims** who eventually settled in what is now the state of Massachusetts. But in the early years of the seventeenth century, these men and women were known as

Puritans. The religious movement known as Puritanism is a direct outgrowth of John Calvin's theology and his quest for a purified form of Christianity—one that has been stripped of corrupt practices, no longer accepts the pope as the head of the Church, and believes the relationship between an individual and God is a strictly personal affair with no need for priests and the spiritual services they provide.

The Protestant Reformation spread throughout the European continent and, in many places, was met with a furious and violent counterattack by religious and political authorities. Across the channel dividing the British Isles from the continent, religion in England was also influenced by the Protestant call for reform. Instead of inspirational leaders such as Martin Luther or John Calvin, however, it was the English king who spearheaded the reform movement.

A farewell meeting is held by a group of English Puritans, before leaving for America, circa 1620.

Portrait of Queen Elizabeth I of England. She ruled the royal realm from 1558 to 1603.

Establishing the Church of England

King Henry VIII was a Catholic monarch who greatly desired a male heir to succeed him. His wife, Catherine of Aragon, a Spanish princess and devout Catholic, gave birth to six children. All of them were girls, and only one—Mary—survived. Desperate to have a son, Henry appealed to the pope to grant him the right to divorce Catherine so that he could marry Anne Boleyn, his mistress and the daughter of a wealthy merchant in London. Pope Clement VII refused the king's request. In response, Henry refused to continue recognizing the authority of the pope in matters of the state.

That was only the beginning of King Henry's decisive break with the Roman Catholic Church. In 1534, he established the Anglican Church, and appointed himself its leader. Henry got his divorce, married Anne Boleyn, and ruled over both church and state until his death in 1547. The Anglican Church, or the Church of England, was Protestant, though it kept the liturgy, some sacraments, and other elements of the Roman Catholic Church.

Queen Mary

Henry's daughter, Mary Tudor, became queen in 1553. A devout Catholic, she undid many of the Protestant reforms and attempted to return England to the Roman Catholic Church. She sentenced to death about 300 men and women who opposed her restoration of the Catholic religion. Queen Mary governed for only five years, but during her brief reign, conflicts within English society threatened to turn into civil war. After her death, Anne Boleyn's Protestant daughter, Elizabeth, became the new queen. She soon recognized that one of her most pressing duties was to bring peace to her troubled land.

Chapter Two

Puritan Separatists of England

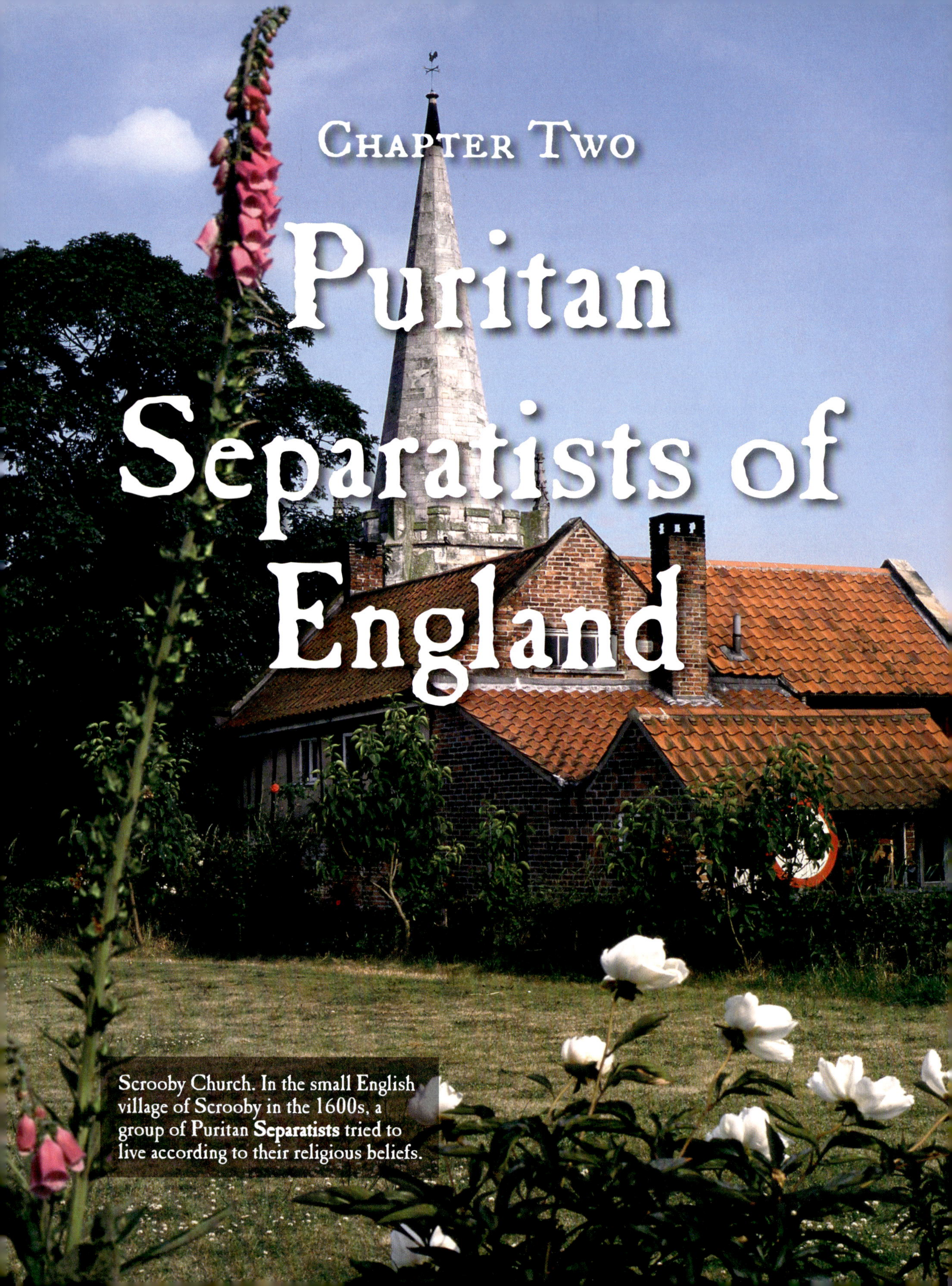

Scrooby Church. In the small English village of Scrooby in the 1600s, a group of Puritan **Separatists** tried to live according to their religious beliefs.

"We, whose names are underwritten, the Loyal Subjects of our dread Sovereign Lord King James having undertaken for the Glory of God, and Advancement of the Christian Faith, and the Honour of our King and Country, a Voyage to plant the first Colony in the northern Parts of Virginia; Do by these Presents, solemnly and mutually, in the Presence of God and one another, covenant and combine ourselves together into a civil Body Politick, for our better Ordering and Preservation."

—FROM THE MAYFLOWER COMPACT, NOVEMBER 11, 1620.

With Catholicism once again the dominant religion in most parts of England, Queen Elizabeth had her hands full trying to reestablish the Protestant Anglican Church as the official Church of England. To accomplish this, she implemented modest reforms in order to avoid angering Catholics. By the end of Elizabeth's 45-year reign, she succeeded in uniting the country and giving her people a common religion—Protestantism. But there were many Protestants who weren't satisfied with Elizabeth's reforms, or with the nature and organization of the Anglican Church. They argued that the Anglican Church, despite its Protestant character, was too close to the Roman Catholic Church. For these critics, the Protestant Reformation in England didn't go far enough. They insisted on a purer form of Protestantism. Because of the position they took with respect to religious reforms, they were called Puritans.

Many English Puritans in the late sixteenth century remained loyal to the Anglican Church, hoping to reform it from within. But some Puritans, taking a more extreme view, believed internal reform was impossible. They were convinced that the only way to practice their faith was by separating themselves from the Church of England and setting up independent Christian communities. These more radical Puritans became known as Separatists, and it was from this branch of Protestantism that the Pilgrims emerged and eventually made a new home for themselves in Britain's North American colonies.

Sailing from England to America

In Scrooby, a small English village in the county of Nottinghamshire, a group of Puritan Separatists hoped to practice their religion and their way of life without outside interference. As followers of John Calvin, the French theologian, they rejected the Anglican Church of England, which they believed was much too Catholic and corrupt. Like Calvin, they believed in predestination and salvation by faith alone. For these men and women, the Christian Bible was their main source of spiritual guidance. They had no use for grand cathedrals or any of the outward signs of religious faith, such as taking part in elaborate church rituals or ceremonies.

For the most part, this group of Christian Puritans was composed of craftsmen, farmers, and some middle-class families. Because their religious ideas and way of worship were outside the mainstream of Protestant Christianity, they had to be careful not to attract the attention of the authorities. Since Henry VIII's break from Roman Catholicism, the Anglican Church and the English monarchy were more or less one and the same. To go against the practices of the Church of England was equivalent to opposing the royal government. Anyone accused of such opposition could be found guilty of treason, and the penalty for treason was imprisonment or death.

To avoid persecution, the Puritans from Nottinghamshire decided they had no choice but to leave England. Between 1607 and 1608, more than 100 men, women, and children escaped to the city of Amsterdam in Holland. Finding Amsterdam incompatible with their way of life and their religious values, they moved to Leiden, another city in Holland, where they stayed for eleven years. Although they enjoyed a certain degree of religious freedom in their new home,

The Pilgrim Fathers boarding the *Mayflower* for their voyage to America. Painting by Bernard Gribble (1872–1962).

these Puritans feared that their children were losing their English nationality and language, and were being wrongly influenced by the permissive ways of Holland's culture.

Once again, this small Separatist group faced the unhappy prospect of having to relocate—but where should they go? They couldn't return to England, and staying in Holland was out of the question. After much discussion, they decided to cross the Atlantic Ocean and seek refuge in England's North American colony of Virginia. Perhaps, in this faraway land, they would at last succeed in creating the community of their dreams and hopes—a place where they could practice their faith without fear of persecution, and where their children could grow up with pride in their English heritage and live according to their parents' Puritan ideals.

Initially, these Separatists planned on sailing to Virginia. In those days, Virginia extended as far north as the Hudson River in what is today the state of New York. Before they could leave Holland, the Separatists needed investors

who would put up enough money to finance their endeavor. They also needed a license from an authorized commercial company. After a failed negotiation with one company, they signed a contract with a group of London merchants. The merchant association agreed to finance their voyage. In return, they expected the Puritan colonists to repay the loan within seven years.

Once preparations were complete, the colonists set sail from Holland's port city of Delft Haven on July 22, 1620. They sailed aboard the *Speedwell* to the English city of Southampton, where a second, larger ship was waiting—the *Mayflower*. On August 5, the two ships embarked on the perilous overseas voyage to the shores of North America. However, the *Speedwell* soon developed a serious leak. Both ships returned to port and waited there until the leak was repaired.

On August 22, the ships set forth a second time, but after crossing 300 miles (483 km) of ocean, the *Speedwell* once again began to leak, forcing both

Signing the *Mayflower Compact*, 1620. Painting by Jean Leon Gerome Ferris (1863–1930).

ships to turn back. The smaller ship was proving to be unseaworthy, so the colonists decided to leave her behind. On September 6, the *Mayflower*, with 102 passengers aboard, set sail alone, departing from the English city of Plymouth.

The voyage took sixty-six days. The sea was fairly calm during the month of September, but in October, the *Mayflower* battled fierce storms. For most of the voyage, the *Mayflower*'s passengers had to stay below deck in cramped, cold quarters, which they shared with their farm animals and personal possessions. Only when the weather was fair and the sea was calm could they come up for a breath of fresh air. The food supply was limited to preserved meat, water stored in barrels, dried biscuits called "hard tack," and dried fruits. One person died during the voyage, and one child was born.

On November 9, at daybreak, the ship's crew spotted land. The Puritans aboard the *Mayflower* had intended to settle along the Hudson River. But the land they spotted was Cape Cod in Massachusetts, several hundred miles north of their destination. They tried to sail south toward the Hudson River, but bad weather and rough seas forced them to reverse course. They sailed around the tip of Cape Cod and spent the next month and a half exploring the coastal area in search of a suitable location to build their settlement.

The license they had received from the Virginia Company in London entitled them to start a colony, or plantation, in the Hudson River Valley. Since they were outside of the Virginia Company's jurisdiction, this first wave of Puritans lacked an external governing authority. Additionally, some of the passengers who were not English Separatists (Puritans) threatened to go their own way.

In order to make peace between the different groups of passengers and to establish an orderly, law-abiding community, the Puritan leaders drew up a document known as the *Mayflower Compact*. It was signed by forty-one adult male passengers and went into effect once a governor was chosen for the new colony. The *Mayflower Compact* was designed to make the colony self-governing. The men who signed this agreement consented to abide by any

Mary Chilton, John Alden, and other Pilgrims landing at Plymouth from the ship *Mayflower* in 1620.

A Difficult Start

The Pilgrims began building their settlement on Christmas Day. By January, winter's freezing temperatures had moved in. In the 1620s, New England winters were much colder than they are now, as the northern hemisphere was experiencing what is referred to as a "Little Ice Age." The Pilgrims also faced a severe shortage of nutritious food, and many became malnourished. By March, forty of the colonists had died, including fourteen of the eighteen women who had made the voyage.

Defending themselves against a possible Native American attack became a frequent worry, especially since the group had lost so many able-bodied men. Whenever an attack seemed imminent, sick colonists were taken from their beds, propped against trees, and given rifles to hold. But, to the surprise of the surviving Pilgrims, local Native Americans chose not to attack. Instead, during the following spring, two spokesmen from a neighboring tribe came to visit and offer help.

future laws and regulations that would benefit the colony. Historians regard the compact as a first step toward democratic government in America—one that is based on the rule of the governed and not the authority of a monarch.

The *Mayflower* reached New England's shore with winter not far behind, and no ready source of food and shelter. To survive the harsh weather, the colonists stayed aboard the ship through much of the winter with none of the comforts they would have enjoyed at home in England. Some of the men went ashore aboard a shallop (a small boat made for shallow water) to explore the land and search for the best location on which to build homes and other structures. During one of their expeditions, they discovered stashes of corn, which the local Wampanoag inhabitants had hidden. (The Wampanoag people were one of many tribes living in the eastern part of New England. The name Wampanoag can be translated as "People of the First Light.")

During a subsequent expedition, they came upon the abandoned remains of a Wampanoag village. On December 11, while exploring the land around Plymouth, the men found what they were looking for—a suitable place to build their colony. The area had running water and fields that had been cleared for planting. The small group of explorers returned to the ship and told the other passengers about their discovery. Toward the end of December 1620, the *Mayflower* anchored in present-day Plymouth Harbor, and the English Puritans went ashore. Their historic landing marked the beginning of England's first permanent settlement in the region we know as New England. The Puritan Separatists, who began the task of creating their ideal community founded on Puritan values and beliefs, are the men and women we call the Pilgrims.

During that first winter in Plymouth Colony, only about half of the settlers survived. The others died from hunger, disease, and exposure to the harsh New

Pilgrims coming ashore at Plymouth, Massachusetts on December 22, 1620. Hand-colored woodcut of a 19th century illustration.

England winter. The following spring, the *Mayflower* set sail for its return trip to England, but those who made it through the winter were not aboard. Despite the suffering they had endured, they were determined to see their dream become reality. They remained in New England and began the difficult task of establishing a community founded on their Puritan faith.

Years before their arrival, English and French fur traders and fishermen had visited the shores of New England and encountered members of various Native American tribes. In 1614, Captain John Smith, one of the leaders of the Jamestown colony in Virginia, explored the area and wrote favorable reports about his experience. Because of its similarity to England, he named the area New England, and hoped his written accounts would attract English settlers. The Puritans who came aboard the *Mayflower* may have been influenced by these accounts.

Chapter Three

Religion in the British American Colonies

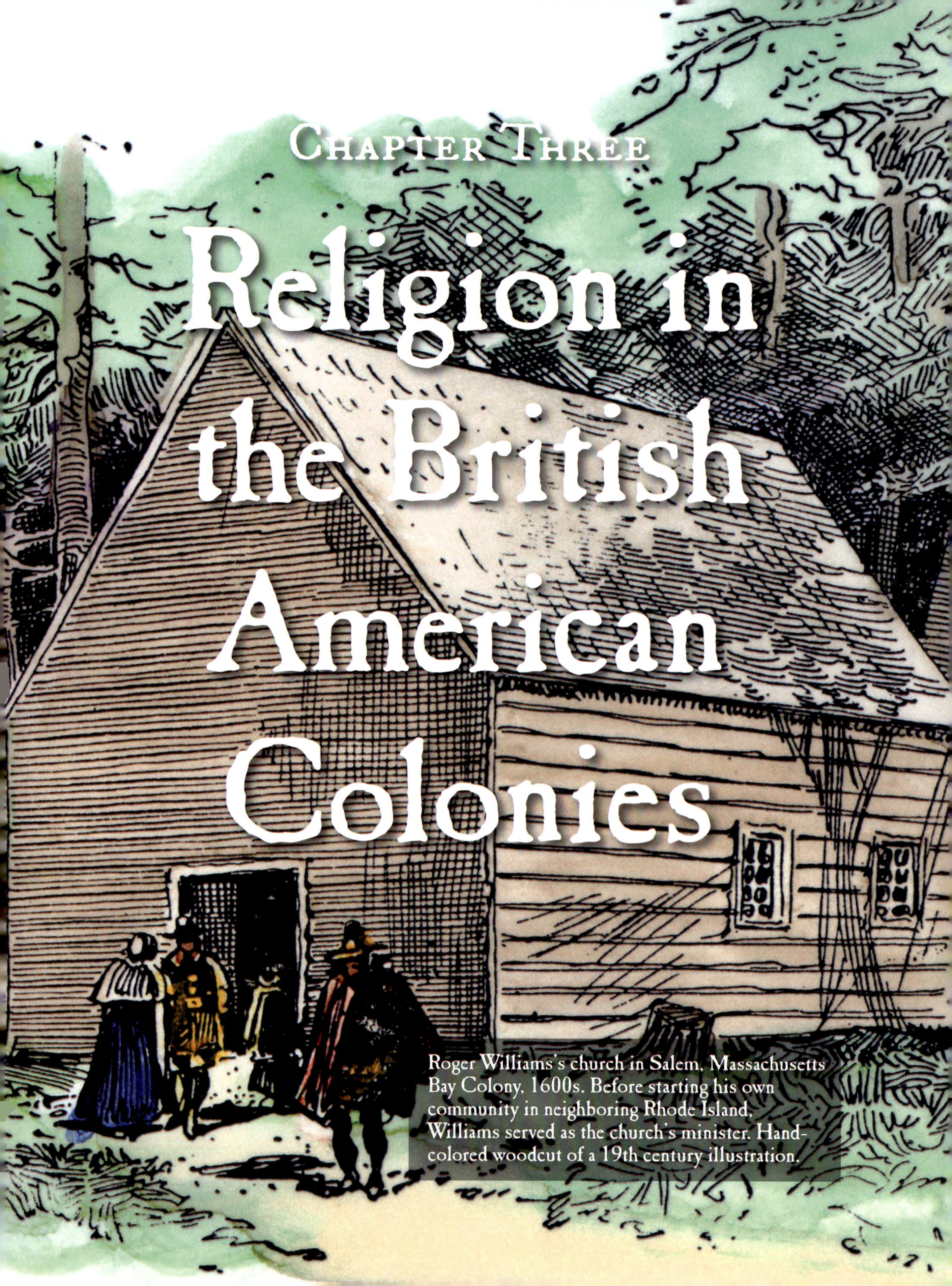

Roger Williams's church in Salem, Massachusetts Bay Colony, 1600s. Before starting his own community in neighboring Rhode Island, Williams served as the church's minister. Hand-colored woodcut of a 19th century illustration.

"The doctrine of persecution for cause of conscience, is proved guilty of all the blood of the souls crying for vengeance under the altar."
—Roger Williams on religious persecution from "The Bloody Tenet of Persecution" (1644)

It took England about 100 years to colonize and develop the different geographical regions along the Atlantic seaboard. England's first permanent settlement in the "New World" was Jamestown in Virginia. Named after King James I of England, Jamestown was officially established in 1607, with Captain John Smith as one of its leaders. By the early 1700s, England had established thirteen separate colonies in North America.

Religious Intolerance in Colonial America

The colonies would eventually break away from England and become the original United States of America. Before that happened, British colonial America extended from Maine to the northern edge of Florida and included three distinct regions: New England, the Middle Colonies, and the Southern Colonies. Throughout the colonial period, Christianity played a central role in each of the colonies. During the opening decades of the 1600s, the colonists faced a variety of obstacles as they struggled to govern themselves according to Christian (Protestant) principles. For one thing, the early settlements were often far apart. Travel between them was difficult and time-consuming, since much of the land was still forested.

Without the benefits of modern communication and transportation systems, religious parishes, or communities, could not easily share information about how they were progressing or problems they were having. The parishes themselves were sparsely populated, with women typically making up only about one-quarter of the population. The number of ministers and other members of the clergy was also fairly low.

In addition to these drawbacks, many people still believed in controversial practices such as astrology, alchemy, and witchcraft, which did not always harmonize with Christian beliefs. (Eventually, the fear of witchcraft would culminate in the Salem trials between 1692 and 1693, when the magistrates of Salem, Massachusetts sentenced twenty people to death for the crime of witchcraft.)

Offender punished by standing in the pillory in a Puritan seaport town, 1600s.

Religious Liberty

Roger Williams founded the colony of Providence Plantation in 1636. Today, we know this settlement as the state of Rhode Island. Williams was born in London, England in 1603. Although he was an ordained minister in the Anglican Church, he felt it was becoming too much like the Roman Catholic Church. In 1631, Roger Williams and his wife Mary decided to leave England, and they sailed to Boston's Massachusetts Bay colony. But Williams' controversial ideas about religion got him into trouble with Massachusetts Bay authorities. When the Massachusetts Court sentenced him to deportation, he fled the colony. Thanks to his friendship with the Narragansett Indians, Williams obtained a tract of land that became the home of the Providence Plantation.

Under Williams' inspired leadership, the new colony granted total religious liberty to all settlers, regardless of their beliefs. The first synagogue in North America, the Tuoro Synagogue, was dedicated in Newport in 1762 but its congregation was established in 1658.

Williams wrote that "Forced religion stinks in the nostrils of God." He also insisted on a complete separation of church and state, established a democratic form of government, and firmly believed that the land of British America did not belong to the King of England, but rather to its rightful owners—the Native Americans.

Because of these and other challenges, the practice of religion in British American colonies was anything but consistent and uniform, even though most of the early colonists were Protestant Christians. Each town, as well as each geographical region, had its own unique religious character, which was greatly influenced by the mix of different ethnic and Christian groups.

Universal religious freedom was never a goal of religious groups who came to the British colonies in America. What mattered to these groups was the right to practice their own particular faith without outside interference or persecution by the government. They had little tolerance for those who held different beliefs. Eventually, eight of the thirteen colonies would have an officially established church, and everyone in the colony was expected to belong to it. People who practiced a form of Christianity that was different from the established religion or who belonged to a non-Christian faith were considered **dissenters**. Such nonconforming individuals could be severely punished for their religious practices.

However, as the population within the colonies increased and the colonies themselves became more settled, a certain level of religious tolerance developed. Perhaps a deeper reason for the growth of tolerance was the arrival of so many diverse groups. Besides the English Puritans and Anglicans, there were **French Huguenots**, Catholics, Jews, Dutch Calvinists, Scottish Presbyterians, Baptists, and Quakers. Without some degree of religious tolerance, it would have been nearly impossible for these various groups to get along with each other, much less maintain their particular identity. In the colonies of Rhode Island and Pennsylvania, by contrast, religious tolerance was more the result of a principled choice than necessity.

Religious Diversity

By the 1700s, the two most important Protestant denominations in British colonial America were Anglicanism and Congregationalism. Anglicans belonged to the Church of England, which kept many of the features of the Roman Catholic Church. In America, Anglicans continued the traditions and practices of their English brethren. For example, they celebrated holy days throughout the year, took part in elaborate religious ceremonies, designed churches with an eye toward inspiring a feeling of holiness, and enjoyed enlivening Sunday worship with music and singing. Unlike Congregationalists, Anglicans did not believe that God had decided in advance who would or would not be "saved" after death. Instead, they taught that salvation was the reward for working hard and leading a virtuous life.

Congregationalists were also Protestant. However, unlike Anglicans, they believed the Church of England had not gone far enough in removing Roman Catholic influences. The Puritans were Congregationalists who settled in

Plymouth in 1620 and later in other parts of New England. Another group of Congregationalists were the Presbyterians (also considered Puritans). Originally based in Scotland, they eventually migrated to the Middle Colonies of New York, Pennsylvania, and New Jersey. The religious philosophy of both groups was based on the teachings of John Calvin, who believed that people are born in a state of sin that can never be forgiven or washed away. Only those whom God has selected will be spared damnation. According to Calvin, these are the "elect" who have been blessed before birth with God's saving grace. For Congregationalists, it doesn't matter how honestly or virtuously a person lives; his or her fate is "written in the stars," or already determined.

In most Puritan communities in British North America, the church was the center of community life, and Sunday (the Sabbath) was the most important day of the week. Religious leaders expected civil authorities to enforce church laws against drunkenness, gambling, swearing, and other vices, especially on the Sabbath. Furthermore, religious leaders also expected the authorities to make sure that everyone attended church on the Sabbath. Puritan church services were solemn affairs that lasted all day. People sat on hard, wooden benches while their pastor or minister read from the Bible and delivered long sermons based on Biblical passages.

The interior of most Puritan churches in colonial America was austere in comparison to Roman Catholic churches. There were no stained glass windows, glowing candles, statues of saints and other holy figures, and no crucifixes or altars. The Puritans who fled England and immigrated to America rejected the ceremonies, rituals, and religious ornaments of both Roman Catholic and Anglican churches. Both groups—Congregationalists and Presbyterians—considered their beliefs and practices to be closer to what they understood as authentic Christianity.

Membership in New England Puritan churches was limited to people who had undergone "**conversion**," a deeply felt religious experience in which they realized they were one of the "saved." Prospective church members had to give a convincing account of their conversion experience. If their testimony didn't include certain telltale signs of a true experience, they could be denied membership.

Church service at Plymouth, Massachusetts, 1600s. Hand-colored woodcut of a nineteenth century illustration.

In the Middle and Southern colonies, there was a greater mixture of religious groups than in Puritan New England. Anglican churches predominated in the South. In Virginia, Maryland, and the Carolinas, the Church of England was the official, state-supported church. In Virginia, where Anglicans were in the majority, attendance at Anglican Sunday worship was compulsory. As more and more Baptists settled in Virginia in the mid-1700s, some Anglican leaders advocated the use of force against them. Baptist preachers were often arrested. Prayer meetings were interrupted. Members of the sect were sometimes attacked.

The colonies of New York, New Jersey, Delaware, and the Carolinas lacked an Anglican majority and were generally more tolerant toward diverse religious groups. Maryland, founded in 1634, started out as a refuge for English Catholics, who were eventually outnumbered by Anglican and Puritan settlers. With this influx of competing faith groups, the Catholics realized it was in their best interests to guarantee religious toleration. For that reason, in 1649, the colony's legislative body passed the Maryland Toleration Act, the second law in the British North American colonies to guarantee freedom of religion to all Christians. (The first such law was passed in the Rhode Island colony in 1635.)

Pennsylvania, one of the Middle Colonies, was founded by William Penn. Penn, an English Quaker, envisioned the colony as a "**Holy Experiment**" in which religious toleration would be the norm. He argued for the separation of church and state, and believed strongly in treating local Native American tribes with fairness and honesty. In 1688, four German Quakers, all recent immigrants to Pennsylvania, publicly declared their opposition to slavery in a written and signed document. This was the first protest against slavery not only in Pennsylvania but also in all of British North America. It read as follows:

> "These are the reasons why we are against the traffik of men-body... Is there any that would be done or handled at this manner? ...There is a saying, that we shall doe to all men, like as we will be done our selves: making no difference of what generation, descent, or colour they are. And those who steal or rob men, and those who buy or purchase them, are they not all alike?"

The men responsible for this courageous act shared the essential Quaker belief that "there is that of God in everyone" and, therefore, all people should be treated equally.

The interior of a Puritan Church was intentionally austere, and didn't have stained glass windows, statues, or an altar.

Chapter Four

Puritanism Takes Hold in New England

Mary Dyer On Her Way To The Scaffold.
Painting by Howard Pyle (1853–1911).

"We shall be as a city upon a hill. The eyes of all the people are upon us so that if we shall deal falsely with our God in this work we have undertaken, and so cause him to withdraw his present help from us, we shall be made a story and a byword throughout all the world."

—John Winthrop

During the 1620s, England experienced a deepening political crisis. In 1625, King Charles I became England's new king. Partly because his wife was Catholic, Charles used his power to make English Catholics more accepting of the Anglican religious faith. For example, he authorized Anglican churches to practice some of the ceremonies and rituals that were in keeping with Roman Catholicism. His father, King James I, had forbidden these very same practices during his reign, in order to satisfy the Puritan wing of Protestantism.

However, Puritans in England also found themselves the target of increasingly oppressive measures under Charles I, including censorship and physical punishment. At the same time, economic conditions in England were showing no signs of improving. The English cloth industry, on which many depended for work, experienced a severe drop in demand. This led to widespread unemployment. Without work or income, many people took to the streets to beg for food or money. To make matters worse, poor harvests pushed up the price of food, and many of the poor died from starvation. Middle-class shopkeepers and property owners feared the worst was yet to come. Some began to think seriously about immigrating to New England, where they might escape poverty by farming large tracts of land.

The Great Migration

Chief among the immigrants were the English Puritans, who were driven not so much by the pursuit of wealth but for spiritual reasons. The year 1630 marked the beginning of what historians describe as the "Great Migration." It was a time when more and more Puritans decided they could no longer remain in the country of their birth. America, they reasoned, would be their new home, and in that distant land they would be free to live according to their beliefs and without fear of persecution. By 1630, the Plymouth colony in New England had become fairly stable and self-sustaining, thanks to a growing population and better harvests.

The colony's achievements inspired a large number of Puritans to make New England their destination. John Winthrop, their leader, had been a Puritan and a prominent lawyer in the English government. He was also a supporter of Puritans who wished to reform the Church of England. His support rankled the government, which had little tolerance for anyone who opposed official policies. Winthrop lost his job and faced the threat of financial ruin for his views on religious freedom and the need for continuing reforms within the Anglican Church. His prospects brightened when he joined the Massachusetts Bay Company, a new business venture based in England. Under Winthrop's leadership, the company voted to establish a new colony in New England.

Building a Bible Commonwealth in Massachusetts

With Winthrop as their newly appointed governor, over 1,000 Puritans braved the Atlantic Ocean aboard a fleet of eleven ships and sailed to Massachusetts. Their trans-Atlantic journey began on March 29, 1630, and lasted about nine weeks. Disease took the lives of some 300 passengers. But those who survived this difficult crossing shared one commanding belief: they were pioneers whom God had chosen to build a "**Bible Commonwealth**." The society they would create in New England would exist as more than a refuge or a beacon of hope to fellow Puritans suffering persecution. It would be a place where the Protestant Reformation would come to fruition, finally free from the corruptions of the Church of England. Moreover, it would serve as a shining example to England and all of Europe of what a free people could achieve when guided by God's hand—and not weighed down by the dictates of church or state.

Many of these migrating Puritans compared their departure from England to the **exodus** of the Israelites from Egypt thousands of years earlier. Like the ancient Israelites, the Puritans thought of themselves as God's chosen people. God had rescued them from bondage at home and expected them to create a community founded on Christian values. After reaching the town of Salem, Massachusetts, in the summer of 1630, they moved first to Charlestown and

Governor John Winthrop of the Massachusetts Bay Colony blessing soldiers holding Samuel Gorton, 1643. After his capture, Gorton was brought to Boston and put on trial for his controversial religious views.

The *Arbella* and other ships bring John Winthrop's colonists to Salem, 1630. Hand-colored woodcut of a nineteenth century illustration.

then to Boston, which would become their new home and the center of the Massachusetts Bay Colony.

Unlike the Puritan Separatists who had established Plymouth Colony ten years earlier, the Puritans of the Massachusetts Bay Colony believed it was still possible to reform the Church of England from within. Separating from the Church was not their goal. What they wanted above all was to build a perfect community in which civil authorities would enforce religious laws and help make sure members of the community led upstanding lives. But achieving such idealistic goals was anything but easy. Soon enough, the colonists of Massachusetts Bay Colony discovered they had different opinions about how the government should be organized, and how their version of Protestantism should be practiced. These disagreements eventually produced major religious and political conflicts that threatened the stability and order of the new colony.

Governor Winthrop was by nature a man willing to compromise and tolerate some measure of religious dissent. However, he strongly believed that too much dissent would destroy any chance of building a Bible Commonwealth in New England. There had to be religious conformity, or his efforts and the efforts of his fellow Puritans would be in vain. For Puritan leaders like Winthrop, religious tolerance was not an option.

Through the decade of the 1630s, the "Great Migration" continued. By 1641, according to some accounts, around 300 ships had carried some 20,000 passengers to New England. As the population grew, the number of settlements also grew, each with its own minister and Congregational church. Most of the immigrants were Puritans from middle-class backgrounds. Newcomers typically passed through Boston, and from there settled in Massachusetts Bay Colony or traveled to other parts of New England in search of land and political and religious freedom. In time, other colonies developed, including Connecticut, Rhode Island, and New Hampshire.

Spiritual Warfare

Puritanism dominated the New England colonies throughout the 1600s. Everyone had to either attend church or pay a fine. In some churches, a man with a long pole carefully observed the congregation. If he caught anyone falling asleep, he might tickle that person's chin with the feathers at the end of his pole. Outside of church, individuals who disobeyed certain moral codes could be whipped, placed in a stockade and publicly humiliated, or even put to death. A particularly grievous offense was practicing or promoting a non-Christian faith or a version of Protestantism that went against the teachings of the local church.

Puritan authorities had no tolerance for Baptists and Quakers, even though both religious groups were Protestant. In 1658, Massachusetts passed a law that made it illegal for Quakers to enter Massachusetts. The penalty for breaking that law was death. Mary Dyer, a Quaker mother of six, had already been banished from the colony for her faith. Despite knowing what would happen to her, Dyer chose to return in order to challenge the religious persecution Quakers endured under Puritan rule. On June 1, 1660, she was hanged from a tree on Boston Common in Massachusetts and became one of four Quaker martyrs.

Puritan authorities believed that any form of nonconformity weakened the community and risked invoking God's anger. In the Puritan worldview, God was very much involved in what happened here on Earth. During the seventeenth century, many New England colonists held to the belief that good and evil were locked in a cosmic struggle for human souls. Even though good would ultimately triumph, people still had to do everything in their power to live by God's laws and not let the devil get the upper hand. To do otherwise was dangerous, since God punished sinners for breaking his laws.

Puritans regarded floods, fires, earthquakes, and other natural disasters as forms of divine punishment. Individuals, as well as entire communities,

The Society of Friends

Mary Dyer and her husband, William, settled in Boston in 1635 where they became members of the Puritan Congregational Church. She became friends with Anne Hutchinson, an outspoken Puritan who challenged the Puritan clergy. Because of her controversial views, Anne was exiled to Rhode Island (Providence Plantation), a colony where dissenters were more than welcome. Sharing Anne's views, Mary Dyer and her family moved with her to Rhode Island, where they lived until 1652. That year, Mary and William traveled to England. After William returned to America, Mary joined the Society of Friends (Quakers). She was drawn to the Quakers partly because of their belief in the equality of women and men, and their belief that the only true authority is God.

In 1656, when Quakers began to emigrate from England to Massachusetts, Puritan authorities passed a number of laws designed to keep them out of the colony. Penalties included whippings, fines, imprisonment, and torture. Two years later, the Puritans passed a more extreme law that condemned to death any Quaker who entered the colony. Defiant to the end of her life, Mary Dyer refused to let the fear of death stop her from living according to her deepest convictions.

believed they could find themselves on the receiving end of God's wrath if they preached heretical doctrines or took part in wrongful actions. According to this perspective, certain types of behavior were signs that the devil was present and doing everything in his power to destroy New England's Bible Commonwealth.

The Salem Witchcraft Trials

Puritans also condemned the practice of witchcraft, which they considered to be the devil's work. In Massachusetts, and in parts of Europe, people believed in magic and the power of witches to do evil. They believed a witch's power came from the devil. Anyone who signed his name in blood in the devil's book would receive magical power. All the devil asked for in return was the signer's eternal soul. In Puritan New England, when children became unexpectedly sick or farm animals behaved strangely, it was surely a sign that someone in their community was practicing witchcraft in league with the devil.

If witches confessed to their crimes, they might be pardoned. But if they refused to admit their guilt, then they could be hung (not burned at the stake, as is commonly thought). Beginning in 1692, in Salem Village, Massachusetts, a wave of witchcraft **hysteria** gripped the townspeople. Many were convinced that witches lived among them and were responsible for all sorts of otherwise unexplainable events. Hundreds of innocent people in Salem and other Massachusetts Bay communities were suspected of being witches. By the end of 1692, twenty people had been convicted and condemned to death for practicing witchcraft. Nineteen of the accused died by hanging; one man was crushed to death under heavy stones. Fortunately, the hysteria passed as people came to their senses and realized how wrong they had been in persecuting fellow New Englanders.

Jeremiads and the Puritan Legacy

In England in 1660, Puritan control of the government ended with the return of the monarchy under King Charles II. With the loss of their power and influence, English Puritans had little choice but to accept their status as a minority within the larger Anglican society. The distant Bible Commonwealth

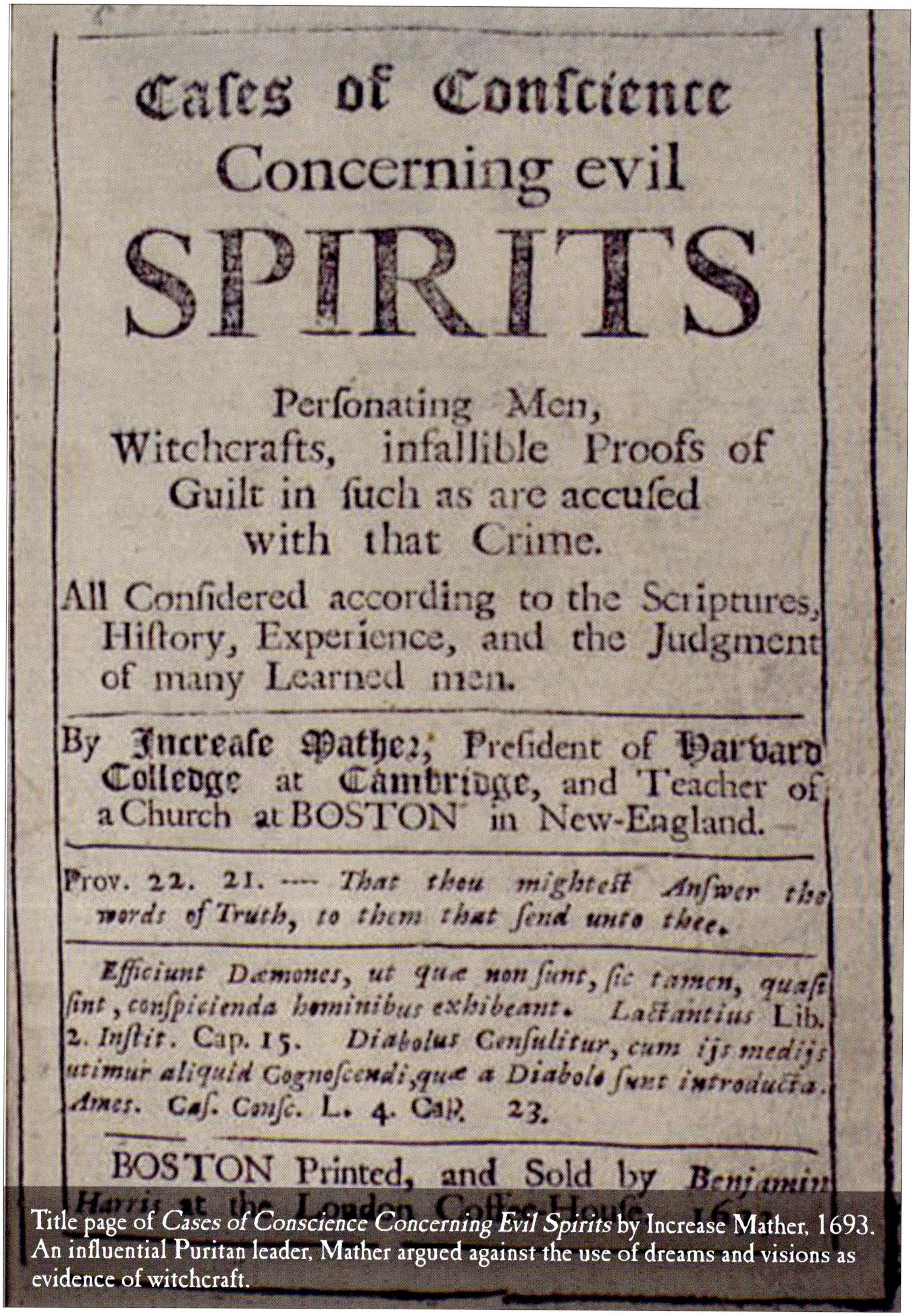

Cases of Conscience
Concerning evil
SPIRITS

Personating Men,
Witchcrafts, infallible Proofs of
Guilt in such as are accused
with that Crime.

All Considered according to the Scriptures, History, Experience, and the Judgment of many Learned men.

By Increase Mather, President of Harvard College at Cambridge, and Teacher of a Church at BOSTON in New-England.

Prov. 22. 21. --- *That thou mightest Answer the words of Truth, to them that send unto thee.*

Efficiunt Dæmones, ut quæ non sunt, sic tamen, quasi sint, conspicienda hominibus exhibeant. *Lactantius* Lib. 2. *Instit.* Cap. 15. *Diabolus Consulitur, cum ijs medijs utimur aliquid Cognoscendi, quæ a Diabolo sunt introducta.* *Ames.* *Cas. Consc.* L. 4. Cap. 23.

BOSTON Printed, and Sold by *Benjamin Harris* at the London Coffee-House. 16[illegible]

Title page of *Cases of Conscience Concerning Evil Spirits* by Increase Mather, 1693. An influential Puritan leader, Mather argued against the use of dreams and visions as evidence of witchcraft.

of New England lost its appeal among many of the Puritans still living in the mother country. For them, the New England colonies had failed to fulfill the dreams of their Puritan founders.

Meanwhile, in the colonies, ministers and other members of the Puritan clergy resorted to a type of sermon called a "jeremiad." They took the name from Jeremiah, a prophet in the Bible's Old Testament. When delivering this type of sermon, the clergy began by naming the many disasters the community had suffered. Earthquakes, war with local Native Americans, floods, and droughts, for example, were not assumed to be random events but God's way of punishing people for having failed to live up to Puritan ideals and falling into sinful, immoral behavior.

But the typical jeremiad didn't end with the minister scolding his listeners for their wickedness. Instead, he reminded them of their brave and high-minded Puritan ancestors who had come to New England to build a model Christian society. Now was the time for the new generation of Puritans to reclaim their heritage and live their lives according to the highest ideals of the Puritan faith.

Some historians argue that in the late seventeenth century, Puritan New England began to decline as Puritanism lost its hold on people. However, this view doesn't take into account the positive impact of Puritan ideals and principles—an impact that has continued into the present. Despite the conflicts with dissenting religious groups and the divisions among the founding Puritans themselves, New England colonists succeeded in creating a stable society and a thriving economy. The Puritan commitment to morality, education, hard work, and religious conviction remains an essential part of American culture.

Chapter Five

Mid-Atlantic Colonies: Religious Diversity and Tolerance

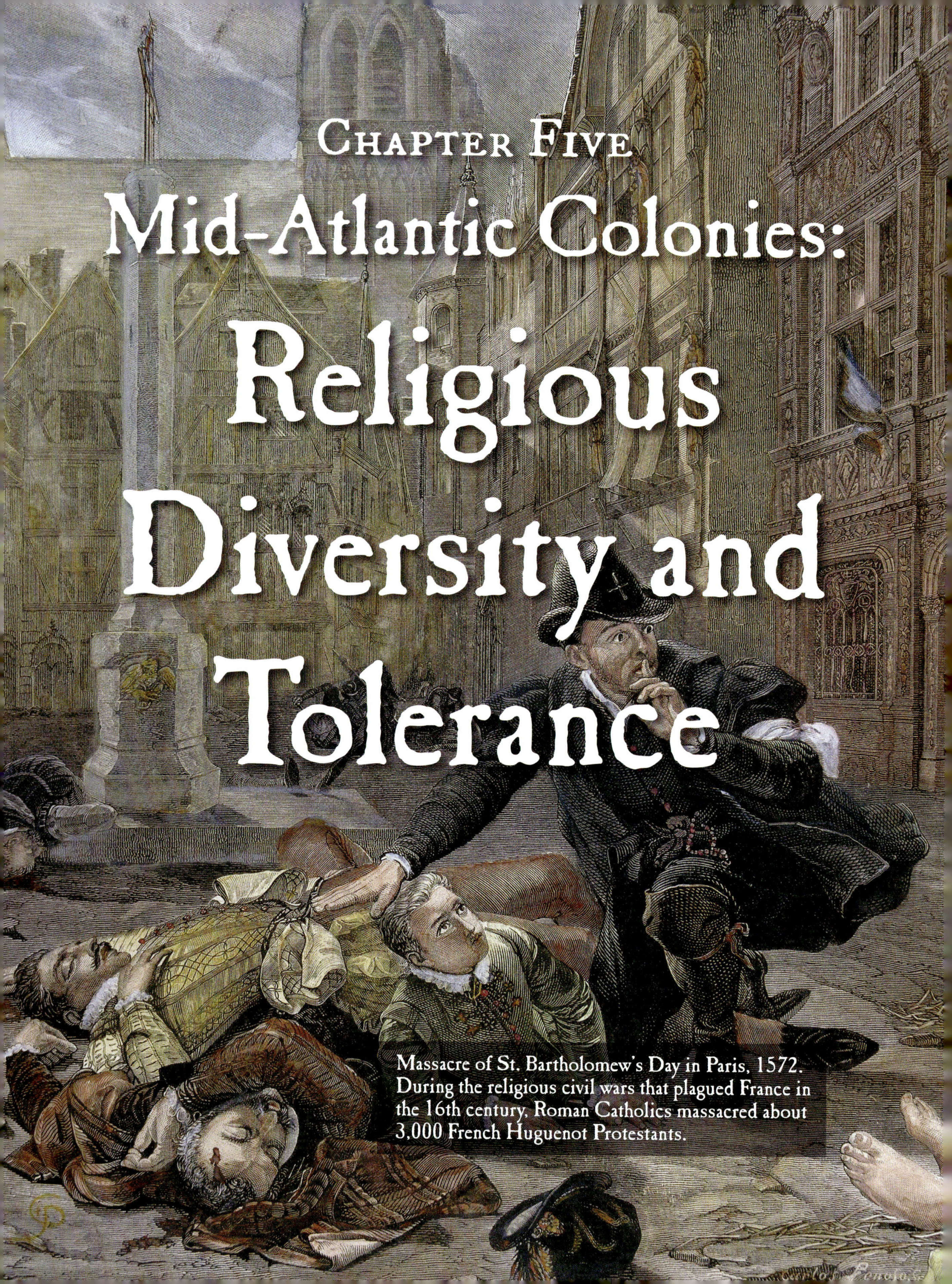

Massacre of St. Bartholomew's Day in Paris, 1572. During the religious civil wars that plagued France in the 16th century, Roman Catholics massacred about 3,000 French Huguenot Protestants.

> "That all persons living in this province, who confess and acknowledge the one Almighty and eternal God, to be the Creator, Upholder and Ruler of the world; and that hold themselves obliged in conscience to live peaceably and justly in civil society, shall, in no ways, be molested or prejudiced for their religious persuasion, or practice, in manners of faith and worship, nor shall they be compelled, at any time, to frequent or maintain any religious worship, place or ministry whatever."
>
> —William Penn Pennsylvania Charter of Liberty, Laws Agreed Upon in England, 1682

The mid-Atlantic colonies in British North America included Pennsylvania, New York, New Jersey, and Delaware. From the start of the colonial era, religious diversity and tolerance were mainstays of life in this region. In New England, most of the early settlers were English Puritans who faced persecution in their native land. They came to America in search of religious freedom to practice their particular brand of Protestantism. Initially, they had little tolerance for other faiths. By contrast, the colonists who settled in the mid-Atlantic colonies hailed from continental Europe. Many were seeking refuge from the religious wars that raged on the continent as a result of the Protestant Reformation.

The Europeans who migrated to the mid-Atlantic colonies represented many different religious traditions, including French Huguenots, members of the Dutch Reformed Church, German Baptists, Portuguese Jews, Quakers, Mennonites, Lutherans, and Anglicans. The region in which they settled included Native Americans and African Americans living and working as slaves. Each of these groups had its own religious traditions, which added to the complexity and richness of mid-Atlantic culture.

Instead of fighting each other over their different religious beliefs, they practiced a "live and let live" way of life. Without a strong degree of religious toleration, the mid-Atlantic colonies would not have survived, much less prospered. But prosper they did, in large part because of their religious and ethnic diversity, or pluralism. In some ways, the society they developed was the forerunner of what would eventually become the United States—a country made up of a vast assortment of different ethnic, racial, and religious groups that have found a way to coexist. By looking closely at a few of the mid-Atlantic colonies, we can better appreciate the role that religion and religious tolerance played in making this region so unique.

New York and the Dutch Influence

Before New York was taken over by the English, it was a Dutch colony called New Netherlands. (The Netherlands is a northern European country also known as Holland.) During the early 1600s, the Dutch became an imperial superpower with a powerful navy, a merchant marine, and a network of colonies around the world. The empire's overseas trade with its colonies, and its control of commercial shipping to and from northern and western Europe, made the Dutch extremely wealthy. The Dutch people enjoyed the highest standard of living in Europe and were not particularly interested in leaving their homeland to settle elsewhere. Unlike the Puritans in England, the Dutch were not persecuted for holding religious views at odds with the official church.

While the English were busy colonizing New England and the Chesapeake region (the colonies of Virginia and Maryland) to the south, the Dutch had their eyes on the mid-Atlantic area, which the English left alone. This area offered many advantages that neither New England nor the Chesapeake possessed. For instance, compared to Maryland and Virginia, the climate in the mid-Atlantic region was much healthier—cooler, less humid, and without the threat of malaria from infected mosquitoes. Unlike the rocky soil found in New

In 1572, under orders from the French court, assassins attacked Admiral Gaspard of Coligny, a Huguenot leader, in his home, while in Paris the St. Bartholomew's Day massacre was underway.

England, the soil was ideal for farming. Plus, the expanses of open land were well-suited to raising herds of cows and other livestock and growing crops like corn and wheat.

The region also had three major rivers, including the Hudson. In the Hudson River Valley, the Dutch established their New Netherlands colony. But under Charles II (whose reign lasted from 1660 to 1685), England was intent on challenging the Dutch empire and reducing its role in America. By now, the English crown understood the importance of developing its colonies as sources of wealth for the mother country. So, in 1664, three British warships sailed up the Hudson River and succeeded in driving the Dutch out of the Hudson River Valley. New Netherlands was renamed New York. Gradually, the Dutch influence lessened as the area acquired a more English character. The victory over the Dutch led to England's development of new colonies in America. Because of their location between New England and the Chesapeake colonies

Quaker founder George Fox talking with women working in a field, 1600s.

of Virginia and Maryland, they became known as the Middle Colonies, or mid-Atlantic Colonies.

As one of the Middle Colonies, New York was home to a variety of religious traditions. The followers of these traditions had their own communities within the colony. For instance, members of the Dutch Reformed Church established themselves in the Hudson River Valley. German Lutherans lived along the Mohawk River, while Congregationalists from New England settled on Long Island. French Huguenots, fleeing persecution in France, founded the town of New Rochelle in the southeastern part of New York. Many of the Huguenots had been craftsmen in the French town of Rochelle.

The Religious Society of Friends (Quakers)

The story of Pennsylvania begins in the middle of the 1600s, when a young Englishman named George Fox set out on a spiritual journey. His parents belonged to the Anglican Church of England, but for Fox, the church failed to satisfy his yearnings for something deeper and more meaningful. He felt the rituals of the church had little to do with real Christianity. He also rejected the need for priests and ministers and the entire structure of church leadership. As he wandered about the English countryside, questioning members of the clergy in his search for answers, Fox began to see a different way of being a faithful Christian. People, he believed, can communicate directly with God, without needing a priest or minister to serve as a "go-between." Furthermore, for Fox, a true church was not a building, no matter how grand or filled with religious symbols.

For Fox, a church is nothing more than a gathering of friends who share a common belief that everyone can have a direct relationship with God. In each person—rich or poor, famous or unknown—there is an "inward Light" that is the sign of God's presence and a source of divine guidance.

In George Fox's time, such notions were considered dangerously radical and contrary to the teachings of the Anglican Church. Despite being imprisoned several times for his beliefs, Fox continued to preach and convert others to his way of thinking. The religious movement he started became known as "Friends of God" or "Children of the Light." Today this unconventional branch of Protestantism is called "The Religious Society of Friends," and its members are called Quakers. In the 1660s, when Charles II came to power in England, the Quakers were targeted for persecution. Many were whipped, jailed, or fined for practicing their religion.

Birthplace of William Penn's Holy Experiment

During this difficult period, a wealthy and well-respected Englishman named William Penn became a prominent supporter of Quakers. His father, a distinguished admiral in the royal navy, was on good terms with King Charles. However, William was not destined to follow in his father's footsteps. In his quest for religious understanding, he came into contact with leading Quakers, including George Fox himself. These encounters, along with William's own natural tendencies, convinced him, in 1667, to become a Quaker and do everything in his power to end their persecution and promote the basic teachings of the Quaker faith.

British statesman and founder of Pennsylvania William Penn (1644–1718) standing on the deck of the ship *Welcome*, bound for America in 1682.

Like George Fox, William Penn found himself in prison more than once for supporting the Quaker cause. In his published writings, Penn attacked the Church of England for some of its doctrines and argued for religious toleration, putting his legal training to good use. When he eventually decided that the English government would never make toleration the law of the land, Penn considered

William Penn's vision of liberating prisoners by removing them from England. Hand-colored halftone reproduction of a 19th century illustration.

establishing a colony in America. It would be a sanctuary for Quakers and other dissident religious denominations—a place where religious toleration and equal rights for all would prevail. He called this ideal society a "Holy Experiment."

Penn knew that King Charles had owed his father a considerable amount of money. Although Admiral Penn had died, William met with the king and offered him a bold proposal: Instead of paying off the debt, why not grant the younger Penn 45,000 square miles (116,000 square kilometers) near the Delaware River in North America's mid-Atlantic region? The king agreed but insisted that the colony be named Pennsylvania ("Penn's Woods"). William Penn wasn't keen on having a colony named after him, since such an honor wasn't in keeping with the Quaker practice of modesty. But the king insisted, and the colony of Pennsylvania was born, at least in name. To build the type of community he envisioned, Penn had a great deal of work ahead of him.

The mid-Atlantic colony would be a "Holy Experiment," similar to John Winthrop's "City on a Hill" but with none of Puritan Massachusetts' religious intolerance. Moreover, in Pennsylvania there would no official church supported by taxpayer money. Even the Quakers would not receive public support in the form of tax dollars. Penn worked tirelessly to attract colonists not only from the British Isles but also from continental Europe. He welcomed Quakers as well as non-Quakers, and promised all newcomers that they would enjoy equal rights.

Penn and the Great Treaty with Native Americans

William Penn, the gentleman Quaker and astute businessman, was well aware that Pennsylvania was not an uninhabited wilderness. He knew of the various Native American tribes who had lived there for centuries. As a committed Quaker, he wanted them to know that he would treat them fairly and never try to take their land by force. Penn wrote letters in English to the leaders of the tribes to assure them that he wished only good relations between them and the settlers. To this end, he offered to obtain Native Ameircan land through fair exchanges of goods. His letters were translated into the local dialects and presented to the "sachems," or chiefs, of the Susquehannock, Shawnee, and Lenape (Le-NAH-pay) tribes.

William Penn didn't stop there. He also took the trouble to learn Native American dialects, so that he would not need an interpreter when negotiating in person. Various artists have depicted him presenting a "Great Treaty" to a group of Lenape Indians in Shackamaxon, near the city of Philadelphia. Historians continue to debate whether a treaty was ever written. What is certain is that for several decades, at least until some of Penn's successors began cheating the Native Americans and stealing their land, settlers and Native Americans maintained fairly peaceful relations. They achieved this by adhering to mutually acceptable terms. These terms were either written down or preserved in oral tradition, and were handed down from one generation of Lenape Indians to the next.

Original Settlers

When the first European settlers arrived in Pennsylvania, they may have imagined the land was a pristine wilderness. But for the Lenape and other Native Americans, the land was their home and had been since the beginning of time. In some translations, the name Lenape actually means "the original people." Like other Native Americans, the Lenape had their own religious beliefs, rituals, and traditions. They believed that a divine being called Kishelemukong created Earth and all living things. They also believed that every living thing has its own spirit, which must be treated with respect. For the Lenape, there was a special spirit who took care of the forest animals and rode through the woods on the back of a deer. This spirit's name was Mesingw.

Stories about William Penn's relationships with the Lenape, Shawnee, and Iroquois tribes became part of both Native American and colonial storytelling histories. Some stories celebrate Penn's participation in Lenape feasts, festivals, and athletic competitions, like foot races and wrestling matches. Other tales recount the genuine affection the Lenape felt toward Penn, even nicknaming him "Brother Miquon." The word miquon means "feather quill" in the Lenape language. (A feather quill is an old-fashioned pen made from a bird's feather. One end is sharpened and can be dipped in ink for writing. Quill pens are what William Penn and other Europeans at one time used.)

Religious Toleration in Pennsylvania

Shackamaxon was where local tribes held their councils. (Shackamaxon is an Native American word that roughly translates to "the place where chiefs meet.") It was also where the first colonists set up their headquarters, or "base camp." Thanks to Penn's shrewd marketing skills, which included writing appealing descriptions of the new colony, Pennsylvania's population rapidly grew. In 1682, William Penn made his first voyage to Pennsylvania. That same year, twenty-three ships from England transported about 2,000 colonists.

William Penn, Quaker and founder of Pennsylvania, meeting with Native Americans to discuss the terms of a treaty.

The following year, 2,000 more arrived aboard twenty ships. Most of the settlers were English Quakers who immigrated with their families to escape persecution in England. But because of the colony's openly declared policy of religious toleration, Pennsylvania attracted members of other persecuted religious sects, such as the Amish and the Mennonites.

While the Quakers were the most prominent religious group, Pennsylvania was also home to large communities of Anglicans, Lutherans, Presbyterians, and other branches of Protestant Christianity. Adding to the religious diversity of the colony were smaller groups of Roman Catholics and Jews. The colony also had its share of African slaves. Many kept the religious beliefs and practices with which they had been raised in Africa, and initially resisted attempts by white preachers to convert them to Christianity.

Quakers were opposed to slavery on the basis of their religious beliefs. However, despite their opposition, William Penn's "Holy Experiment" did not include universal freedom. Slavery still existed in the colony. Penn himself owned at least three slaves, who lived and worked on his country estate, called Pennsbury.

By 1730, the colony had imported about 4,000 slaves to work as domestic servants and laborers in the city of Philadelphia and surrounding areas. In 1780, Pennsylvania passed the Gradual Abolition Act, which required the steady phasing out of slavery. Pennsylvania was one of the first states in the Union to pass such a statute. By 1790, there were about 10,000 African Americans in Pennsylvania, but by then the majority (about 6,500) had been granted their freedom.

Religious toleration in Pennsylvania meant that non-Protestant groups were entitled to practice their faith without fear of persecution. However, these groups were limited in other ways. For instance, non-Protestant groups did not have the right to vote or to hold political office. These rights did not extend to Muslims and Jews because, in their religions, Jesus Christ was not recognized as the savior of humanity. Roman Catholics were also prevented from voting and holding political office mainly because they continued to regard the pope as the head of Christianity.

Chapter Six

Southern Colonies: Dominance of the Anglican Church

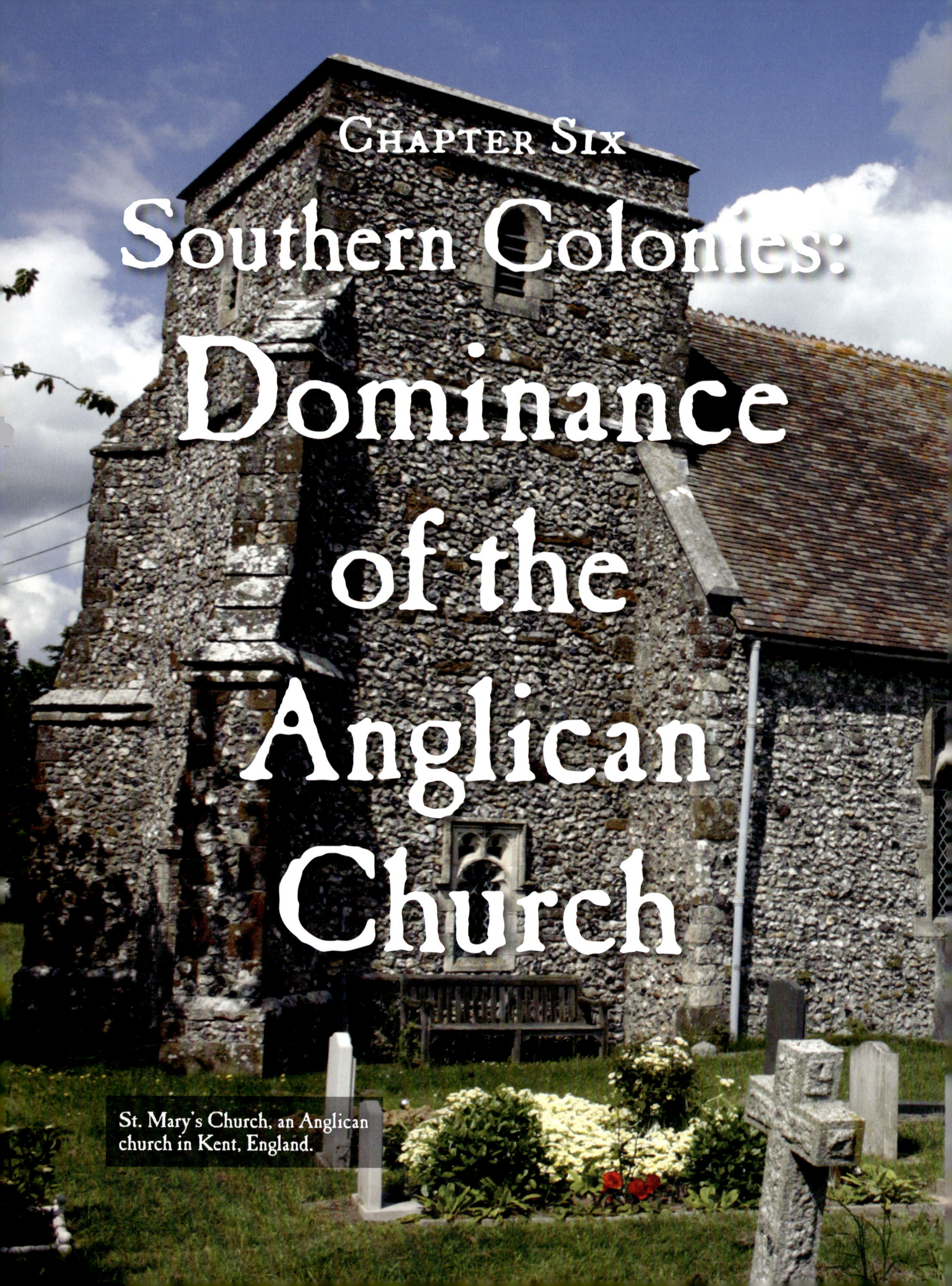

St. Mary's Church, an Anglican church in Kent, England.

"The legitimate powers of government extend to such acts only
as are injurious to others. But it does me no injury for my
neighbour to say there are twenty gods, or no god.
It neither picks my pocket nor breaks my leg."
—THOMAS JEFFERSON, 1781

Most of the Puritans who came to America in the seventeenth century were not seeking religious freedom. What they wanted was the freedom to practice their own religion. Puritans believed their religion was the truest form of Christianity. They had very little tolerance for those who practiced a different form of Christianity, such as Catholicism, or a non-Christian faith such as Islam or Judaism. People who disagreed with Puritan beliefs and practices were not welcome in New England and could be banished or even executed. Puritan Separatists, like the Pilgrims, came from a land where Protestants and Catholics were killing each other because of their different interpretations of Christianity. During the sixteenth and seventeenth centuries, much of Western Europe, including the British Isles, endured bloody conflicts over religious differences. These religious wars, which often developed into general wars, increased poverty, unemployment, crime and political and social instability. In the Thirty Years' War (1618–1648), which began as a fight between Catholics and Protestants, the population of what is now Germany was reduced by 30 percent.

Government-supported Religion

Because of so much turmoil, many people in Europe, and England in particular, believed that government should take sides and give its full support to one denomination or the other. They argued that an established, state-supported church would ease rising social and political tensions, and help build a stable, peaceful society. Christians who migrated to North American colonies to escape persecution and social unrest wanted the same thing: an established, government-supported religion that would serve to cushion them against chaos. Puritanism (also known as Congregationalism) was the official religion in the New England colonies—except for Rhode Island—through much of the seventeenth century.

In the southern British American colonies, by comparison, the Church of England became the dominant religious institution by the end of the seventeenth century. Anglicanism is the Protestant denomination associated with the Church of England—the established, or official, church in England. In Virginia, the colonial government passed a law requiring everyone to attend an Anglican church. Those who didn't attend were considered dissenters and could be subject to fines or imprisonment. The government used a portion of its tax revenues to cover the cost of maintaining church property, and to pay the salaries of the clergy. This was common practice in the other southern colonies where the Church of England was the official church.

Where Persecuted Catholics Found Peace

Maryland's history during the colonial era followed a different path. The colony was founded as a refuge for Catholics who had been persecuted in England for their beliefs. In 1632, King Charles I of England granted George Calvert (the first Lord Baltimore) the rights to all the land between the Potomac River and the Chesapeake Bay. Two years later, his son, the second Lord Baltimore, began the process of colonizing this land both as a refuge for Catholics and a source of economic wealth for himself and his descendants. (The King named the territory "Maryland" in honor of his wife, Queen Henrietta Maria.)

However, most of the early settlers in Maryland weren't seeking religious freedom. They wanted to profit from the colony's farming potential. Like Virginia and the Carolinas, Maryland possessed rich, fertile fields ideal for growing exportable crops such as tobacco and rice. The first wave of colonists included both well-to-do English **aristocrats**, who were mostly Catholic, and laborers and craftsmen, who tended to be Protestant. Since large-scale agriculture requires a large workforce, there were also a growing number of Protestant immigrants who were willing to accept low wages as farmhands.

Maryland politicians realized that if Protestants were in the majority, Lord Baltimore's dream of creating a sanctuary for Catholics would be doomed. In time, Anglican immigrants as well as Puritans outnumbered the Catholics. To prevent the Church of England from exercising control over the colony and its Catholic settlers, Maryland's General Assembly, in 1649, passed the Act Concerning Religion (later renamed the Act of Toleration), which assured religious freedom to all Christians. Part of this law reads as follows:

> [N]o person or persons whatsoever within this province... professing to believe in Jesus Christ shall from henceforth be in any ways troubled, molested, or discountenanced for or in respect of his or her religion, nor in the free exercise thereof...

Five years later, Puritan lawmakers in Maryland succeeded in repealing the Act of Toleration. But in 1661, a more enlightened General Assembly restored the Act, which remained in force until 1692, when a new English governor arrived in Maryland. Appointed by King William III (an Anglican monarch), he outlawed religious toleration and made the Church of England the official church of Maryland. Moreover, English laws intended to suppress Catholics remained in force until the American Revolution. Separation of church and state was made the law of the land in the First Amendment to the United States Constitution, which begins with the following clause: "Congress shall make no law respecting an establishment of religion..."

African American enslaved workers picking cotton on a southern plantation in the nineteenth century.

Africans in Colonial America

The economy in the Southern colonies depended largely on agriculture. Because of the South's warm climate, long growing season, and fertile soil, the region could produce abundant crops of tobacco, rice, and cotton. But the job of planting and harvesting these crops required many workers. Instead of hiring workers and paying them a decent wage, growers with large farms (known as plantations) turned to the trans-Atlantic slave trade as their primary source of cheap labor. Also called the triangular trade, this globalized system of **exploitation** lasted from the sixteenth to the nineteenth century and connected the economies of Europe, America, and Africa. A French historian, Jean-Michel Deveau, has described the slave trade as one of the "greatest tragedies in the history of humanity in terms of scale and duration."

Between 1450 and 1850, at least 12 million African men, women, and children were taken forcibly from their homes, packed aboard ships, and sold as slaves in the "New World." About 90 percent of Africans were taken to the islands of the Caribbean and South America. The other 10 percent were sold throughout the North American continent. The South was not alone in using enslaved Africans to keep the economy going. British colonies in the North also relied upon the slave trade. Northern business owners put Africans to work as slaves in a range of industries including shipbuilding, sail making, sawmills, iron foundries, and in rum-making plants. Overall, roughly 25 percent of the colonial population in both the North and the South owned slaves.

Historians estimate that about 20 percent of Africans brought here from Central and West Africa were Muslims, whose religion was Islam. A much smaller percentage was Christian. Catholic missionaries were already present in Africa before Christopher Columbus's voyages to the New World in the 1490s. The majority of enslaved Africans, however, had their own religious beliefs and ceremonies, which they attempted to keep alive in America, instead of converting to Christianity. But their initial resistance to conversion began to lessen when they encountered **evangelical** Christianity. This form of worship felt much more compatible with the traditions they had followed in the past.

African Influences

Africans who came to America as slaves represented many different cultural groups. Each group had its own language, customs, and religious beliefs. Holding on to these beliefs under the terrible conditions of slavery was an unending struggle. Many of the slaves came from West African societies, where people believed in a Supreme Creator in addition to lesser gods. They were expected to honor these gods, as well as their ancestors and elder members of their community.

West Africans hoped to maintain a healthy balance between the spiritual world and the visible world around them. During their worship ceremonies, they incorporated dance, singing, and storytelling. In Colonial America, as West Africans and other African people came into close contact with Christianity, they blended elements of the Christian religion with their own beliefs and rituals. The result was the beginnings of a distinctively African American expression of Christianity.

Chapter Seven

The Great Awakening and the Rise of Evangelism

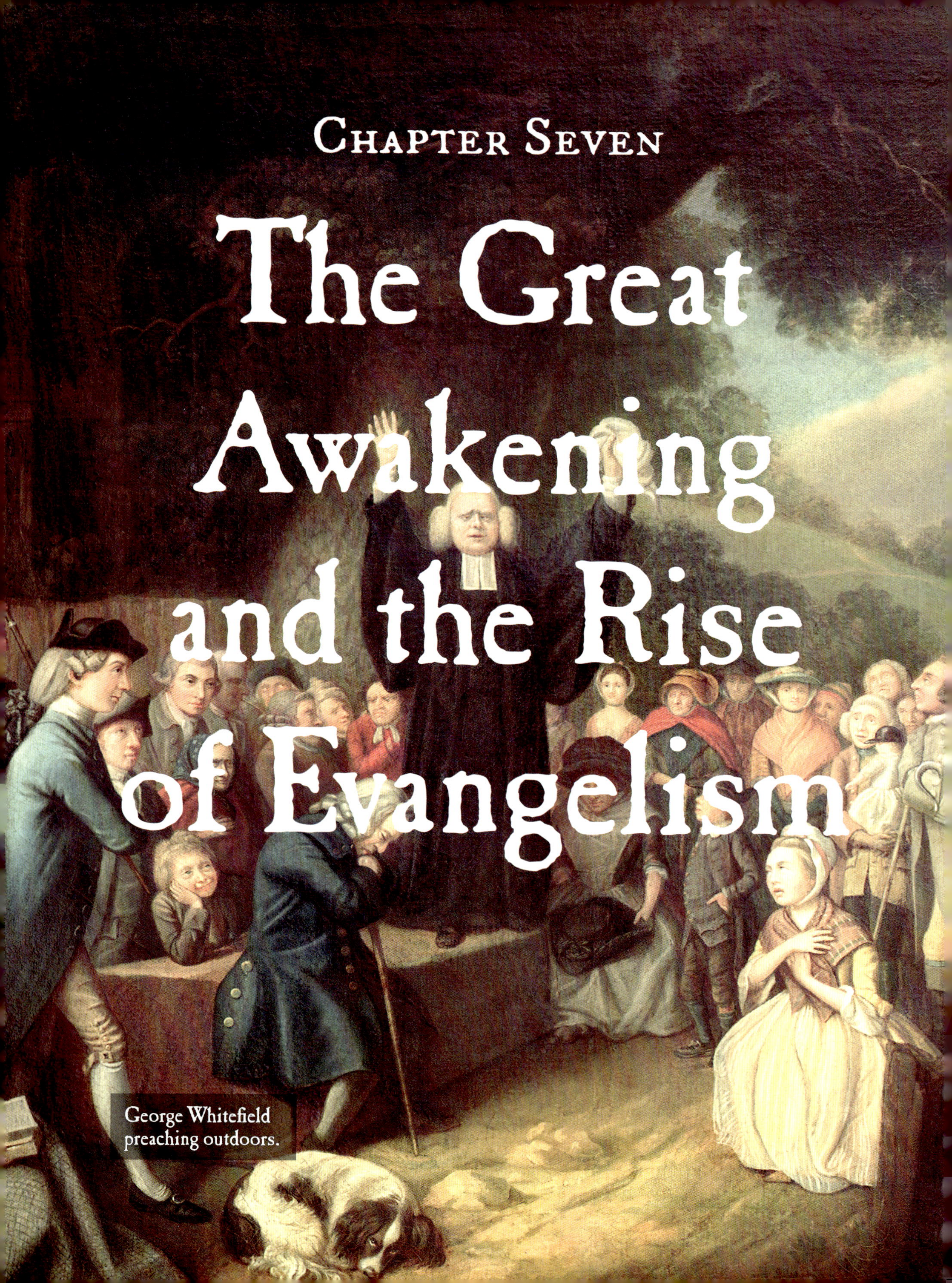

George Whitefield preaching outdoors.

"He makes less of the doctrines than our American preachers generally do and aims more at affecting the heart. He is a born orator. A prejudiced person, I know, might say that this is all theatrical artifice and display, but not so will anyone think who has seen and known him."

—Sarah Edwards, wife of preacher Jonathan Edwards, on preacher George Whitefield

From the 1730s through the 1770s, religion in colonial America experienced an infusion of energy and excitement. This revival of the way people practiced their faith has been called the **Great Awakening**. For a new generation of preachers, God was not a distant, divine being removed from human affairs but a living, breathing presence who cared deeply about all his children and took an active interest in their daily lives. Because religious revivals tended to draw large crowds, the meetings were often held outdoors.

Revivalist preachers felt that too many people were not taking their Christian beliefs seriously. They also criticized Anglican and Congregational churches for giving dry, academic sermons that appealed more to the mind than the heart. Another reason for the Great Awakening was the changes occurring in American culture. Many felt that churches were becoming too worldly, overly concerned with acquiring property and wealth—instead of attending to spiritual matters.

For many Protestants in the American colonies, going to church became an emotionally charged experience. In contrast to the austere atmosphere of

Puritan worship, a revivalist-style service, provided outlets for people's feelings. It unfolded as an exciting theatrical event in which everyone could participate, and it served as a spiritual counter to the Age of Enlightenment.

The historian David Blight describes one such gathering:

> ...There had never been anything like it. Here's a meeting of 3,000 people out in a field, blacks and whites together, listening to a preacher who says, "Here in my message is a new life for you, here's a new chance for you. Here's a God who had your interest at heart. Here's a God who may deliver you."

People who attended these services experienced a spiritual depth and a feeling of closeness to God missing from the traditional church. What's more, they felt a genuine sense of fellowship with other worshipers—the feeling that came from sharing a common experience. In many ways, revivalism in colonial America would live on as evangelical, or "born again," Christianity in the United States. This form relies more on biblical revelation than on science or reason.

George Whitefield

New England colonists knew about Whitefield's novel style of preaching and the large crowds he attracted in England. In 1740, when he arrived in Boston, he was welcomed as something of a celebrity. His religious passion inspired him to travel throughout the colonies, from north to south. In one year, he covered over 5,000 miles (8,000 km) and gave about 350 sermons. On Boston Common, roughly 25,000 people listened to him preach. Similarly large crowds turned out for his appearances in Philadelphia and New York City. His preaching was so heartfelt that audiences responded by weeping, crying out, and even fainting from the intensity of their feelings. With his flamboyant style, charismatic personality, and emotional sermons, Whitefield is credited with having sparked the Great Awakening in colonial America.

George Whitefield preaching in London, 1642.

Revivalism Crosses the Atlantic

The first wave of the spiritual renewal called the Great Awakening happened in England in the seventeenth century. Toward the end of the 1600s, a few charismatic ministers, such as John and Charles Wesley and George Whitefield, felt that people had grown too comfortable with the Anglican faith and that the religion itself had lost its dynamic core. They adopted a more dramatic, spontaneous style of preaching that wasn't limited to a church setting. Reverend Whitefield, for example, delivered his sermons not only in churches but outside in fields, on streets, and even while sitting on his horse. Using his background in theater, he electrified crowds with his passionate sermons, which he gave with all the flair and drama of a trained actor. Along with the Wesley brothers and other Anglican ministers, Whitefield set in motion a religious revival that led to the founding of the Methodist church, a Protestant denomination, and the rebirth of religious fervor in colonial America.

The Great Awakening spread from New England to Georgia, thanks to the work of George Whitefield and his followers and converts. Revivalist, or evangelical, meetings were especially attractive to small farmers, tradesmen, laborers, and impoverished whites who had little religious background. They also appealed to black people. Religious gatherings that recognized human equality and encouraged people to express openly their feelings of joy or sorrow—this was a form of Christianity they could accept and embrace.

New Lights Versus Old Lights

Of course, not everyone was pleased with how the Great Awakening was changing the way people practiced Christianity. Conservative clergymen throughout the colonies objected to revivals on the grounds that they made people unruly and disruptive. They also frowned upon the tactics used by

A black preacher addressing his mixed congregation on a plantation in South Carolina, c. 1860.

evangelical preachers, which they felt were far too emotional and sensational. Another aspect of the Great Awakening that troubled these ministers and other church officials was the apparent breakdown of social order. In their eyes, people had to know their place in society and who was above or below them on the "social ladder." They were appalled by evangelical services, where everyone was on an equal footing.

Because of these and other objections, by the 1740s, many congregations and entire denominations were divided into separate camps. Those who opposed the Great Awakening were known as the "**Old Lights**." Those who endorsed this religious revival were the "**New Lights**." The conflict became so intense that revivalist factions within large churches formed their own independent Protestant denominations. The Anglican and Congregational churches had been the major religious groups in the colonies. But as a result of the Great Awakening, their membership began to drop as more and more people joined the new evangelical groups.

The Great Awakening led colonial churchgoers to question, perhaps for the first time, the authority of church leaders. They also questioned the hierarchy of the church, in which power flowed downward from the leadership to the people. Some historians argue that the changes occurring in the practice of religion during the eighteenth century influenced what was happening in the larger society. Change was in the air. People were becoming dissatisfied with British interference in the colonies. If they could challenge the authority of their church, then why must they defer to the authority of the British king? Didn't they have every right to rebel and form a government of their own . . . "of the people, by the people, for the people"?

Could there be a direct link between the Great Awakening and the American Revolution, which came decades later? On April 19, 1775, British troops battled members of an armed colonial militia in Lexington, Massachusetts. Perhaps the people who had lived through the Great Awakening and experienced liberation from religious authority were among those who now wanted political independence as well.

Glossary

aristocrats
Wealthy, privileged members of a society's upper class.

Bible Commonwealth
The name John Winthrop gave to the ideal Bible-based society he hoped to create in the Massachusetts Bay Colony in the 1630s.

bureaucracy
The record-keeping system used by large organizations and institutions to organize and keep track of their affairs.

conversion
In religious terms, a deeply felt personal experience in which the individual undergoes a sequence of powerful emotions. These emotions are connected with the person's awareness of himself as a sinner who is helpless to change his fate. The conversion experience is one of spiritual rebirth and a transformed sense of the world.

disciple
A person who follows the teachings of a highly respected political or spiritual leader.

dissenters
Individuals who practiced a non-Christian faith or an unacceptable form of Protestantism.

evangelical
A form of Protestant Christianity in which the acceptance of Jesus Christ is regarded as the way to personal salvation.

exodus
The departure of a large number of people from one place to another.

exploitation

The unjust, selfish use of a person for someone else's private advantage or gain.

French Huguenots

Protestants in France in the sixteenth and seventeenth centuries who suffered persecution for practicing their faith.

Gospel

Any one of the four narratives concerning the life and death of Jesus Christ in the Bible's New Testament.

Great Awakening

The evangelical religious movement that originated in England but soon swept through the British American colonies beginning in the early 1700s. The movement was inspired by unconventional ministers who used a more emotional style of preaching that had great appeal.

heretics

The label attached to people whose theological beliefs are considered false by religious authorities.

Holy Experiment

The ideal society William Penn hoped to establish in the Pennsylvania colony in the seventeenth century. Penn envisioned a society in which Quakers and other nonconforming religious groups could practice their faith without fear of persecution.

holy relics

The preserved artifacts or remains of a saint or other officially recognized holy person, such as Jesus Christ or a saint.

hysteria

An outburst of extreme emotion and feelings of panic.

indulgences

In Roman Catholicism, indulgences refer to the power of the Church to cancel part or all of the punishment a person will receive for his sins after death. Indulgences are not forgiveness for the sins, rather they are incentives to live more in accord with the teachings of the Church. Martin Luther objected more to the abuse of indulgences than to the indulgences themselves.

New Lights/Old Lights

In eighteenth-century colonial America, New Lights were thepeople who supported the rise of evangelical Christianity during the period of the Great Awakening. Old Lights were people who rejected this more exuberant form of Christianity.

Parliament

The law-making body of the British government, comparable in many ways to the United States Congress.

Pilgrims

Puritan Separatists who sailed to America aboard the *Mayflower* in 1620 and established the first permanent colony in New England.

predestination

A concept taught by John Calvin (1509—1564), a French scholar who left the Roman Catholic Church and joined the movement for re-form. His doctrine of predestination teaches that God has decided in advance what will happen to people after they die. For Calvin, doing good works while alive was no guarantee that a person would be saved.

Protestant Reformation

A sixteenth-century religious revolution that began as an attempt to reform the corrupt practices of the Roman Catholic Church. Influenced by men like John Calvin and Martin Luther, the Reformation led to the creation of Protestantism as the third major branch of Christianity.

Purgatory

According to Roman Catholic doctrine, Purgatory is the place where some saved souls go after death. To enter Purgatory, a person's sins must be forgiven. The purification he or she receives in Purgatory prepares the soul for eternal life in heaven.

Puritans

English Protestants who believed the Church of England was too close to Roman Catholicism. Puritans sought a "purer" form of Protestantism.

sacraments

In Christianity, sacraments are religious ceremonies that Jesus Christ is believed to have established during his lifetime. In the Protestant Church, the two most important sacraments are baptism and communion, which celebrates the Last Supper Jesus is said to have had with his disciples.

salvation

In Christianity, salvation is a religious concept that means a person has been saved from the consequences of his or her sins—the breaking of God's laws.

Separatists

English Protestants who rejected the Church of England. Instead of working to reform the Church from within, they aimed to establish independent religious communities where they could practice their faith.

sin

In Christianity, a person commits a sin when he or she deliberately breaks one of God's laws or disobeys God's will.

theologian

An expert in the study of religion.

Further Reading

Nonfiction

Burgan, Michael. *African Americans in the Thirteen Colonies*. New York, NY: Children's Press, 2013.

Butler, Jon. *New World Faiths: Religion in Colonial America*. New York NY: Oxford University Press, December 31, 2007.

Grigg, John A., *ed. British Colonial America: People and Perspectives*. Santa Barbara, CA: ABC-CLIO, 2008.

Rubin, Julius H. *Tears of Repentance: Christian Indian Identity and Community in Colonial Southern New England*. Lincoln, NE: University of Nebraska Press, 2013.

Taylor, Alan. *Colonial America: A Very Short Introduction*. New York, NY: Oxford University Press, 2013.

Fiction

Atkins, Jeannine. *Anne Hutchinson's Way*. New York, NY: Farrar Straus Giroux, 2007.

Fraustino, Lisa Rowe. *I Walk in Dread: The Diary of Deliverance Trembley, Witness to the Salem Witch Trials*. New York, NY: Scholastic, 2011.

Gunning, Sally. *Bound*. New York, NY: William Morrow, 2008.

Reese, Celia. *Sorceress*. Somerville, MA: Candlewick Press, 2009.

Speare, Elizabeth George. *The Witch of Blackbird Pond*. Boston, MA: Sandpiper, 2011 (originally published in 1958).

Online Information

Colonial America (1492–1763)
The Library of Congress
www.americaslibrary.gov/jb/colonial/jb_colonial_subj.html
From the Library of Congress in Washington, D.C., this kid-friendly website offers young readers an engaging look at America's past, including true stories about the country's colonial era from 1492–1763.

Diving America: Religion in American History
TeacherServe, National Humanities Center
nationalhumanitiescenter.org/tserve/divam.htm
From the National Humanities Center, this website features a well-organized collection of information on religion and influence on American culture from the seventeenth through the twentieth centuries.

Plymouth and New England Colonies
Chronicles of America
www.chroniclesofamerica.com
This website is designed to bring each phase of America's development into sharper focus by providing such information as religious influences, as well as culture, government, and geographic facts.

Selected Bibliography

About Martin Luther. Public Broadcasting Service. www.pbs.org/empires/martinluther/about_relu.html.

Africans in America: Religion and Slavery. Public Broadcasting Service. www.pbs.org/wgbh/aia/part2/2narr2.html.

BBC-History-Ancient History in Depth: Christianity and the Roman Empire. British Broadcasting Corporation. www.bbc.co.uk/history/ancient/romans/christianityromanempire_article_01.shtml.

Bierhorst, John, ed. *The White Deer and Other Stories Told by the Lenape*. New York, NY: William Morrow and Company, Inc., 1995.

The Church of England in Early America. TeacherServe, National Humanities Center. nationalhumanitiescenter.org/tserve/eighteen/ekeyinfo/chureng.htm.

English Dissenters: Puritans. Exlibris. www.exlibris.org/nonconform/engdis/puritans.html.

The English Reformation. British Broadcasting Corporation. www.bbc.co.uk/history/british/tudors/english_reformation_01.shtml.

Facing History and Ourselves. Mary Dyer: "Yea, and Joyfully I Go." . nobigotry.facinghistory.org/content/martyrdom-mary-dyer-"yea-and-joyfully-i-go".

God in America: People: The Protestant Reformation. Public Broadcasting Service. www.pbs.org/godinamerica/people/protestant-reformation.html.

Gray, Edward G. *Colonial America: A History in Documents*. New York, NY: Oxford University Press, Inc., 2003.

"History & Archaeology: God, Government and Roger Williams' Big Idea." *Smithsonian Magazine*. www.smithsonianmag.com/history-archaeology/God-Government-and-Roger-Williams-Big-Idea.html?c=y&page=2

John Calvin. Calvin College. www.calvin.edu/about/john-calvin

Mary Dyer: A Colonial Execution. Awesome Stories. www.awesomestories.com/biographies/mary-dyer/life-in-puritan-massachusetts.

Moore, Susan Hardman. *Pilgrims: New World Settlers & The Call of Home*. New Haven, CT and London, England: Yale University Press, 2007.

Peace Treaty. Penn Treaty Museum. www.penntreatymuseum.org/treaty.php.

Religion and the Founding of the American Republic: Religion in Eighteenth Century America. Library of Congress. www.loc.gov/exhibits/religion/rel02.html.

Religion in American History: African American Christianity. TeacherServe, National Humanities Center. nationalhumanitiescenter.org/tserve/nineteen/nkeyinfo/aareligion.htm.

Religion in 18th Century America: Lesson 1: The Great Awakening. EDSITEment. edsitement.neh.gov/lesson-plan/first-great-awakening#-sect-background.

Encyclopedia Britannica Online, s.v. "Roman Catholocism" www.britannica.com/EBchecked/topic/507284/Roman-Catholicism.

Roman Catholic Origins, Roman Catholic History, Roman Catholic Beliefs. www.patheos.com/Library/Roman-Catholicism.html.

The Southern Colonies. U.S. History. www.ushistory.org/us/5.asp.

Taylor, Alan. *American Colonies*. New York, NY: Viking Penguin, 2001.

Theopedia, an Encyclopedia of Biblical Christianity. *95 Theses*. www.theopedia.com/95_Theses.

Quotation Sources

Introduction: Early Christianity

p. 5, Quoted at gbgm.unc.prg/umw/bible/Milan.stm.

Chapter 1: The Protestant Reformation

p. 11, From a 1545 essay by Martin Luther, quoted at europeanhistory.boisestate.edu/reformation/luther/22.shtml.

Chapter 3: Religion in the British American Colonies

p. 29, Statement by Roger Williams, quoted at www.pbs.org/wnet/historyofus/web03/segment2.html

p. 33, The Germantown Protest (1688), quoted at www.yale.edu/glc/aces/germantown.htm.

Chapter 4: Puritanism Takes Hold in New England

p. 35, A statement from John Winthrop, quoted at http://www.goodreads.com/author/quotes/519465.John_Winthrop.

Chapter 6: Southern Colonies: Dominance of the Anglican Church

p. 59, Teaching American History in Maryland, quoted at teachingamericanhistorymd.net/000001/000000/000005/html/t5.html

p.59, U.S. Constitution—Amendment 1, quoted at www.usconstitution.net/xconst_Am1.html.

p.60, Transatlantic Slave Trade/United Nations Educational, Scientific and Cultural Organization, quoted at www.unesco.org/new/en/culture/themes/dialogue/the-slave-route/transatlantic-slave-trade.

Chapter 7: The Great Awakening and the Rise of Evangelism

p. 64, Africans in America/Part 2/Religion and Slavery, quoted at www.pbs.org/wgbh/aia/part2/2narr2.html.

p. 67, The Gettysburg Address by Abraham Lincoln, quoted at www.abrahamlincolnonline.org/lincoln/speeches/gettysburg.htm.

Index

Author Biography

George Capaccio is a poet, storyteller, and writer. A native New Englander, he graduated from the University of Massachusetts with a Bachelor of Arts in English literature. Since he began writing for children and older students, Capaccio has written fiction and nonfiction on a variety of topics—such as the sun and the planets, the nervous system, America's historic highways, and even what life was like during the Middle Ages.

Though born into the Roman Catholic faith, Capaccio has been a longtime attender at Friends Meeting at Cambridge (Quaker) in Cambridge, Massachusetts. While writing this book about religion in the British American colonies, he discovered his experience with Quakerism was invaluable. Cappacio's research also led him to new discoveries about George Fox, the founder of Quakerism, and renewed his interest in the colonial era. He now plans to develop a storytelling program of nonfiction stories about the life and times of people who lived during that period.